"Words Fail Me"

How

language

works and

what

happens

when it

doesn't

PRISCILLA L. VAIL

MODERN LEARNING PRESS
ROSEMONT, NJ

Permissions

Thanks to Robert MacNeil for his gracious permission to use a section from his eloquent and entertaining book, *Wordstruck.*

I have been wrestling with, studying, dreaming about, lecturing and writing about, experimenting with, analyzing, noodling around with, messing about with, and trying to grasp the topics addressed in this book for over forty years. Thus, those who have come along with me on my written or spoken journey may recognize a few signposts, phrases, or schemas. While some may seem familiar, I have given myself permission to develop them in new ways, setting them in the context of current research and knowledge. They, like the other ideas in this book, are my talismans and my familiars.

P.L.V.

ISBN 1-56762-062-0

Dedication

To
Donald Vail,
who has shown me
wealth of expression
with
economy of words.

Acknowledgements

Thanks to The Book Group, outgrowth of "The Tape Deck," for expanding to include me. Assigning books so rich in language lets me abandon my New England conscience and immerse myself in the power of words, guilt-free, in the morning or when there are still dishes in the sink. The Sentence is a joyful discipline, the discussions are never dull, and the treasured camaraderie is a gift in this busy world. For these liberties, luxuries, and challenges I am grateful to, in alphabetical order: Barbara, Betty, Kate, Mandy, and Penny.

Thanks to our children, in order of age, whose life stories and braveries give delight and enlightenment: Melissa, Polly, Lucia, Angus.

Thanks to our grandchildren, *per stirpes*, for sharing the joy of youth and the wisdom of the ages: Luke, Thomas, Jesse, Willa, Jack, and Melissa.

Thanks to the Orton Dyslexia Society, collectively, for the knowledge, research, and wisdom they offer.

Thanks to Margaret Mayo-Smith and Ned Hallowell who, working singly for dual purpose, try to sharpen my thoughts and blunt my foolishness.

Thanks to Robert Low, *sui generis*, my editor.

Priscilla L. Vail
Stonington, Connecticut
August, 1995

Contents

Introduction
Learning Words to Use, Using Words to Learn

A Luncheon Companion

Errors are windows. Kids show us their thoughts through their words.

One day last fall, I saw my third grade friend, Brett, walking down the hall. I've had my eye on him more than he realizes.

"How goes it?" I asked.

"Great! You want to have lunch at our table?" he offered.

"I'd love to. Say, what's for lunch today?"

"Pizza and *skin* milk," he said.

"I love pizza," I replied, "but what's *skin* milk?"

"Same as the other kind, I guess, but it just comes from a different part of the cow."

This invitation to cheesy cholesterol and liquified hide came from the heart, and from the language which informs the heart and the mind.

As is so often true, humor illuminates serious situations. We can all laugh at the prospect of *skin* milk. But, the results of flawed language are not amusing: skewed concepts, mismatched ideas, words which are slippery instead of stable, mirages of meaning, and hollow expression.

Issues

Why do kids need language, how do they get it, how do they use it, and how are they hampered without it? Why is language in jeopardy in today's noisy, verbal culture? What should adults do?

If we ignore the situation, we will fit the title of this book: *Words Fail Me.* If we heighten our awareness of How Language Works and What Happens When It Doesn't, we can help students with Learning Words to Use and Using Words To Learn.

Preview

This book has ten chapters, organized in a one-to-ten progression and followed by a conclusion, a Resource Section, and an index. Condensing a subject as multi-faceted as language into a numerical schema is perilous. Readers bristle. "Seven Rungs? I could think of ten." This plea for reader charity comes from a writer who is trying, without being proprietary, to give manageable, enticing, explanatory shape to a subject everyone else already owns.

What of a reader who becomes interested in a topic—perhaps wordplay—and thinks, "All very well, but how do I help?" Lists of applicable books, sources of materials, and further readings are in the Resource Section. Also, each chapter ends with a section called "So what are we supposed to do about all this?" which provides brief descriptions of techniques, games, and strategies. But, this book is not a *how-to*; it's a *why-we-must.*

Imperative

In the Information Age, people of all ages need powerful and precise verbal tools, yet many young people are neither acquiring the words they need nor expanding their existing linguistic capacities. Collectively and individually, we cannot afford this impoverishment. For our society to function, for people to make productive use of the tidal waves of information available through electronics, we need the skills of sorting, prioritizing, and organizing which language offers. For individuals to participate and grow, we need well-honed communication skills.

Humans are unique among species in the way we are wired for language. Words, in solitary thought or in exchange, give us power to think, express feelings, acquire information, organize thought, anticipate the future, make peace with the present, and remember the past. Language takes us on intergalactic journeys to invisible kingdoms. It is ours; we owe it protection and use.

One Capacity
Language, The Passepartout

I asked twelve children, ranging in age from four to twelve, "Why does language matter?"

They answered:

"So you can tell your Mom what you need."

"You can understand what the Doctor tells you to do if you're sick."

"Unless you had language, you couldn't have ghost stories."

"To get the joke."

"You use it to make friends and share."

"It's the other half of music."

"It helps you pretend to be any person, and takes you anywhere in time and space in books or stories."

"So you can investigate whatever you want."

"Simple. Communication."

"People couldn't understand without it."

"Can't think without it."

"Because you want to understand what other people want you to know. Then, you don't just keep on saying 'what?'"

Short on grammar, long on punch, these kids are sampling the delights of a unique human capacity: language.

Language is a key to information, emotion, past experience, current happenings, or future goals. In its own glorious manner, it can describe itself in a word: *passepartout.* This elegantly Victorian expression, meaning a key of universal access, derives from the French *passer* (to pass, go, or travel) and *partout* (everywhere). A passepartout, which rhymes with "glass o' bar brew" or "lass, far few," unlocks doors to imagination and reality, comedy and tragedy, insight and knowledge, wisdom and mystery.

Alarmingly, though, many of today's infants, children, students, and people of all ages don't have keys and aren't learning to be locksmiths. Those whose language doesn't develop beyond rudimentary levels are limited to immediate personal experience, in the individual context of the present moment: "I want it now."

Think how many vital parts of social contracts depend on understanding "if...then..." (In addition to the social realm, "if...then..." is an essential building block of computer programming.) *If* is an artifact of language. That we cannot see, touch, feel, taste, weigh, or throw *if* doesn't diminish its power. The basic concept of cause and effect builds from this and other linguistic foundations. Kids with weak language face serious academic, social, and emotional penalties.

"Balderdash!" a grandfather said to me. "Kids make just as big a racket as they ever did. Talk too much, not too little, if you ask me." Yes, kids' jaws are hinged and their vocal cords vibrate, but what types and levels of language have they absorbed, and what, reciprocally, do they give out?

Too few take in language in its robust and subtle glories. As a result, too few can give out language with strength and complexity. For an alarming number of people—young and old—existing keys rust or bend, the skeleton key is a phantom, locks jam, escutcheons fall aslant, hinges freeze, knobs come away in the hand, sills buckle, jambs warp.

To a new and frightening extent, this happens among the affluent and impoverished; over and under-populated; rural, urban, and suburban. The blight crosses the four points of the compass, both genders, and living generations. Language impoverishment closes off access to thoughtful reflection, just when our needs for communication are escalating.

What follows applies to preschoolers up through college students and on into professional echelons. Those who have missed early language levels have lacunae in their thoughts and concepts. Like the blind lady's knitting—whose stitches may feel nicely placed along the needle—holes and gaps invade the fabric.

Some readers will be primarily interested in young children. Many will be launching emergent readers and writers. All will know people across the life span whose weak language—often misinterpreted as low intelligence, lack of interest, or self-absorption—has held them back.

Whatever the ages of the people we teach at school, raise at home, collaborate with at the workplace, or bury in the churchyard, responsible nurture requires understanding where their language came from, its reliability, and its trajectory.

Involuntarily and unconsciously, from motives sinister, noble, or just plain lazy, our culture has traded linguistic nourishment for verbal fast food. We nosh, like, on the Golden Arches of McLanguage.

We gulliblespeak: buzzwords. We discountstorespeak: slogans. We sirenspeak: ads. We sneakspeak: flat tax. We liespeak: politics. We verbspeak: impact. We bloatspeak: utilize. We bulgespeak: "vehicle placement supervisor" for parking attendant. We psychobabble: I feel the real you, searching for your personal best in your personal space. We diminishspeak: Using the standard formula for assigning grade levels to reading materials, we must peg *cogito ergo sum* at second grade because it is a three-word sentence.

How did language start to slip? Who cares? What's next? Where to begin?

How did language start to slip? Some of us didn't notice. Others did but couldn't control the slide. But, we can control on an individual basis how we use language. A combination of apparent efficiency, habit, social pressures, and lack of vigilance got us where we are. We weren't trying to do bad things; we didn't understand the importance of what we were letting slip. Because we have all continued making sounds, we didn't notice that some expressed content but others were air bags.

Who cares? Every member of our society, sharing our present and shaping our future, needs to care. In the world beyond childhood, complex issues cry for exploration at the same time they are spawning problems. Quick fixes are dangerous and usually temporary. Oversimplification makes molehills out of mountains. We only reach complexity of thought through our capacities to listen, interpret, connect, infer, and question, then to dispute, defend, and discuss. Only through language can we hold two opposing ideas in mind simultaneously—comparing, contrasting, and evaluating. Language allows us to buy into ambiguity without selling out. But, weak, shoddy, slippery language lures us into the Disinformation Age.

At home, linguistic appetites form early and habits stick. Kids copy parents and siblings. The point is too obvious to belabor.

At school, with budget-driven drifts to larger class sizes, diminished staff, outdated materials, and inadequate supplies—not to mention inclusion and philosophical warfare over the teaching of reading—language development becomes an invisible victim. Language belongs to all, and all are diminished when some are impoverished.

What's next? This small book, based on neurological research, classroom experience, and common sense, explores how to use words to learn and learn words to use. The examples and strategies which follow come from schools, carpools, parent conferences, teachers' successes, and grandparents' breakthroughs. The situations are real and the suggestions, by and large, FREE!

Where to begin? Humans have the capacity to understand and manipulate symbols. Symbols are arbitrary representations; they are not the objects themselves. My dictionary says, "Symbol: That which stands for or suggests something else...a visible sign of something invisible...an arbitrary or conventional sign such as a character, a diagram, a letter, or an abbreviation used instead of a word or words, as in math, physics, chemistry, music, phonetics, or the like..."[1]

These are all written symbols. But, long before people get to reading and writing, they enjoy the commerce of heard and spoken symbols—trading, assessing, and valuing words. We will explore the relationship between receptive and expressive language in the next chapter, Two Strands. Here is the place to lay the groundwork for that later investigation.

Human children absorb words through exposure. According to Rockefeller University's George Miller, "...for many years after starting to talk, a child learns new words at a rate of more than 10 per day," arriving at high school with a vocabulary in the neighborhood of 80,000 words. This collection includes extensions of single words (*love: loves, loved, lovable, unlovable, lovably,* etc.), proper nouns, names and places particular to individual experience, and words whose meaning is inferred, often through process of elimination.

For example, writing in Scientific American, Miller and Gildea give the example of color words. In an experiment, they first determined that a group of three-year-olds did not know the word for the color *olive*, calling it *yellow, green,* or *brown,* but they did know *blue, red, yellow, brown,* and *white.* They put two trays in front of the children, blue and olive, and asked each child to "hand me the chromium one, not the blue one." Inference and process of elimination worked in all cases. A week later, asked to name the colors of five trays, they couldn't remember the term *chromium* but didn't mislabel it as *yellow, green,* or *brown.* As the authors point out, "A single exposure was enough to begin a reorganization of their color lexicon." [2]

As young children learn the meanings of *cookie, no, ball, go, car, up, bath,* they string these words together into intelligible combinations by using grammar. Although the bitter, hot controversy still boils in some quarters, such highly regarded language researchers as Steven Pinker believe that humans arrive on earth wired with an innate, though dormant, grammar system. This system emerges as the child learns words and begins to communicate with others. Preschool children aren't "taught" grammar any more than they increase their vocabularies by looking up words in the dictionary. Expanding vocabulary demands increasingly complex organization; vocabulary and grammar grow apace.

The language-learning child also develops "inner speech." Through what's called The Vygotsky Fusion (named for the Russian linguist, Lev Vygotsky) "thought becomes fused with language and thereafter they develop together." [3]

Inner speech slips out as the child plays, the painter works, or the writer writes. Observing a child with a toy truck, we might hear, "Here's the bad guy. Vroom, vroom. Here's the good guy. Faster. Smack-up. Crash. Here's the police."

The child isn't inviting any participation. He is attaching words to thoughts and actions, tying them together in a primitive kind of narrative. It's a self-satisfying way to order thought. Far from reaching out to others, the child immersed in inner speech would be perplexed and probably annoyed to have another join in his personal activity. In fact, our listening to audible inner speech is a form of eavesdropping.

Inner speech is lifelong: the patterns formed in childhood continue into adulthood. As I am writing this, the painter in our house is replacing door hardware on the newly repainted woodwork. He holds a plastic cup of assorted screws, and I hear him saying, "OK. This must be it. No. Wait. This guy's got yellow on him..." He doesn't know I hear him using inner speech to pick through the bits of hardware. When an adult's inner speech is audible, we say, "Odd duck, Joe. Talks to himself, you know."

Working on an earlier section of this chapter, I was stuck for a verb. I fished around in my head. No luck. I went for a walk, had a cup of tea. Still no luck. Returning to my keyboard, I snagged the perfect word. "Yes!" I cried out. "Yes. Yes. Yes. I love it!" My husband, downstairs, called up, "Congratulating your best friend again?"

As vocabularies expand and grammatical structures proliferate, we use what I think of as "Adjust-a-Speak." We use different voices, rhythms, rates, complexities, and vocabularies for our various audiences, relying on such adjustments to help us hit the bull's eye. A little granddaughter, here for a visit, has used a wide variety just in the space of an hour. She talks in an admonitory way to her doll, with level-playing-field language to her brother, in a wheedling way to her mother, shyly with a lot of silent head nodding to my friend on the phone, and in the boisterous language of executive planning to her friend, who is coming over later for a playdate.

"Motherese" is the simple vocabulary, slow cadence, and voice warmth that loving adults—be they high school dropouts or rocket scientists—use with babies. "Oh, there. Good girl. Here we go. She's a hungry girl. Oooo. Easy now. What a good baby."

Those with a variety of lexical levels can match their words to their listeners, shifting formality, vocabulary, decibel, slang, and content according to the situation.

The nursery school teacher of a wild-minded, rampaging student may say to a parent after a turbulent six weeks, "Things are settling down."

The kid trying to give herself courage to go off the high dive says, "I can do it!"

I heard a mother of a teenage daughter wail to her friend, "I've totally blown it. Now we'll be a dysfunctional family for sure! You know how Miranda has been the past couple of months? Yeah. She's been Madonna, right? So last night I said goodnight in Madonnaspeak, and when she came down this morning I said good morning the same way. The trouble is that overnight she turned herself into Ruth Bader Ginzberg."

Words and letters aren't our only symbols system: logos help us locate products; international signs show us to the airport restroom and tell us when not to turn left. Chemical notations tell us the ratio of hydrogen to oxygen in water (H_2O). Maps and compasses, giving us latitude and longitude and NESW, help us find our way; we journey through cartography. The numbers and the hands on a clock, the names of the days and the months, and the numbering of the years are our symbols system for recording and anticipating the sequential journeys of our lives. Twelve o'clock is a symbol, nothing more. Expressed 12:00 A.M. or P.M., noon or midnight, it has no magic of its own; but its power to evoke is enormous:

Clefs and other musical notation help conductors keep order and tenors keep on track:

Numerals, process signs, decimal points, fraction bars, and equal signs help us navigate the kingdom of mathematics. Perhaps this is the place to reinforce the distinction between mathematics and arithmetic. Arithmetic demands accurate retrieval of factual information and tidy pencil/paper skills. Mathematics is a language and a symbol system which allows us to ask the questions which unlock the secrets of how our universe is ordered.

Thus, if language gets off track, it isn't only *Words Fail Me;* other disciplines, too, move out of reach.

So what are we supposed to do about all this?

1. Acknowledge the benevolent and malevolent power of symbols: the Red Cross and the Swastika.

2. Provide examples and open doors. In exercising our remarkable capacity for language, humans try to tame the forces

of time and space, explore the mysteries of mathematics, tap the wellsprings of emotion, and share individual and collective stories.

3. Usually, language unfolds as it is needed and emerges as a way for us to illuminate new needs. However, sometimes the process goes awry. We need to know what to notice in assessing adequate or insufficient language development. When the language system doesn't develop smoothly, we need to understand the particulars, predict their likely consequences, build in prevention as well as remediation, and offer precise help as opposed to free-floating, buckshot bolstering.

4. Parents are the first alarm system, followed by teachers. Sadly, most pediatricians, parents' first advisors, are notoriously cavalier: "Don't worry, he'll grow out of it," or "Einstein didn't talk until he was four, and he turned out OK." This is poor advice. Children seldom "get better on their own." Language problems need to be pinpointed and addressed early in life. Subsequent chapters will show how.

5. We'll see examples from the borderline between adequate and aberrant, along with strategies for help. We will also see some serious language weaknesses and consider ways to offer on-target help. Children thus afflicted seldom find joy in academics or deep fulfillment in later life. Our charge to monitor this aspect of development brings with it serious responsibilities.

6. Yet, the worst approach is one of doom and gloom. We need to remember that a light touch goes far; humor is as much a part of language as syntax.

7. Our journey through this book will show us normal development, which—just because it's normal—doesn't deserve to be left to fend for itself. It, too, needs attention and nurture.

8. We need to cultivate our own active love of language, which provides contagion.

9. We need to remember the power of the storyteller, and the power of story to predict as well as to record. Without language, stories vanish. Anthony Bashir says, "We become the story of who we tell ourselves we are." Adults tell children who they are all the time, and perhaps because we are taller and more experienced, they take us seriously. Kids model their own stories of who they are on the models we give them. Through language, kids can tell themselves and others the stories they hope will come true.

10. Heightened awareness, diligence, and our own delight in language will help us regain the passepartout and bequeath it to the children entrusted to our care, opening wide the doors to learning, living, loving, and laughing.

Two Strands
Receptive and Expressive Language

What They Are

Language is made of two strands: receptive and expressive. Receptive language is what the child takes in; expressive is what the child produces. These two intertwine in language development. They fit the metaphor of seed and crop.

The condition of the soil; the amount of sun, shade, and water; and the number and variety of seeds and bulbs planted determines what will sprout, blossom, bear fruit, give aesthetic delight, and provide physical nourishment. If we take the time to remove rocks, till, mulch, furrow, fertilize, and water, we increase our chances that what we plant will come to life. If we blow dandelion fluff across hard, crusted soil, we will harvest a sparse crop of dandelions. And, if we want variety and nourishment, we don't dump a whole envelope of marigold seeds in a single hole, or crowd all our seeds, bulbs and transplants together. Knowing which varieties of flora and food will bring pleasure and sustenance, we sow, bury, cover, water, and wait.

What They Need

Receptive language—the seeds and bulbs of the child's linguistic crop—needs preparation, planting, and patience. If we want an assortment, we will plant perennials and annuals, flowers and vegetables.

Expressive language—as it sprouts—needs room for growth, thinning, staking, mulching, weeding, encouragement, and a watchfully protective eye.

Receptive Language

Receptive language capacity grows from birth or even before. The normal infant hears sounds and begins to distinguish environmental noises from human voices—which are near or far, to the right or left, male or female, adult or child. After the child has learned to smile, we see dramatic evidence of the power of a voice: hearing a parent coming home and saying, "Where's my beautiful big girl?" the baby will wave its arms, wriggle, smile, and one day crow with delight.

The baby listens intently to the stream of conversational sounds. One magical day, the child recognizes a phrase or word, realizing that a particular collection of sounds is familiar and always means the same thing. *Cookie, Mama,* or *soooo big* are constant, no matter who says them. This is the child's first step into the symbolic kingdom of language and the infinite space of communication.

Junkie-joyful, the child gathers up and absorbs whatever words, sentences, voices, rhythms, inflections, and modulations are around. Indiscriminate and insatiable, the child absorbs the linguistic atmosphere. If grunts or grumbles are all that is floating around in the air, the child will grow a grunt and grumble collection. If single words are stretched out for easy listening (*haaaaappy baaaaaby*), if voices lilt, if laughter floats, and if songs soothe, the seeds of vigorous and vibrant language begin to grow. This process continues throughout childhood and adulthood. All through life, the quality of the language we absorb enriches or impoverishes the caliber of our output.

What we receive through hearing is also groundwork for what we will understand and enjoy in reading. Reading is a kind of listening with the eyes.

Kids who grow up hearing tangles of short sentences and canned laughter—TV talk—aren't learning the sustained attention required for understanding explanations, directions, narrative, or abstract reasoning. They are not growing the linguistic variations which prepare them to read history, literature, philosophy, or *Gone With the Wind*. High school kids whose music lyrics are limited to "Babuh, Babuh, I wanchoo, Babuh," are planting mental crabgrass; hard to remove and destructive of gentler species. Small children, middle-size children, and huge children (sometimes called adults) who balance their verbal intake with narrative, humor, endearment, purpose, mystery, and information are planting a "garden of earthly delight."

The young child isolates the words, phrases, and individual sounds which rumble around in speech. The child with an intact receptive language capacity will hear them accurately, in correct sequence, and will remember as well as understand. The learning child recognizes emotional content, gathers information, makes connections, and in sorting lexicons, readily distinguishes the fairy tale from the commercial, or a poem from a scolding. In tumbling growth come the differences between declarative sentences and questions, active and passive constructions (there's a big difference between "the girl *hit* the boy" and "the girl *was hit* by the boy"), figures of speech (raining cats and dogs), simile (as gentle as a fawn), metaphor (Ellie is the fawn of the family), and analogy (fawn : deer :: colt : horse).

But, some children—from underexposure or from weakness in the language system—don't accomplish all those wonderful, seemingly simple goals. They hear inaccurately ("The Bible tells about Adam and *Even.*"), they tangle sequence ("I saw an *ephelant.*"), they forget what things are called ("Hand me the *thingy.*"), or their words betray misunderstanding ("I had a *handburger.*"). A *handburger* combined with a glass of *skin* milk is a recipe for trouble!

Expressive Language

Babies are generous—they try to give back to the world the sounds, words, and flowing speech they have heard. Thus, long before the child can actually talk, we hear lilted, inflected babbling. It sounds real. We bend closer, smiling. The baby smiles back and continues. We shake our heads, unable to understand, but we smile and offer encouragement, and the baby keeps on practicing, learning to "sing" long vowel sounds, making unintentional Bronx Cheers (is this politically correct?), and playing with repetitive strings of consonants. One fine day and—sad to say—probably by accident, the baby stumbles on the combination "Da-da." The world stops. People flock to see and hear. The father puffs with pride: "Say it again." The mother leans closest, coaching, "Ma-ma." What has happened in this tableau?

A young experimenter has serendipitously hit the jackpot: the world is his for the taking—or, rather, talking. The kings, queens, princes, and princesses of his land bend near, smiling, hoping for more. The baby, being an active learner, tries again as the onlookers offer models for him or her to copy. Here is the start of active conversation. Here is the pay-off for having paid attention to all those strings of sound. The combination of memory and mimicry wins the day. Children launched in such a way keep on listening, learning, trying, and talking. If older people in the child's life ignore or try to silence their experimentations, children lose heart—their expressive language puts out few shoots; may wilt or wither altogether; bear small, bitter fruits; or be barren.

No matter what age children are when they start to develop expressive language, the progression unfolds as follows:

- gesture
- labels
- two words
- morphology
- syntax
- semantics.

Let's consider each of these levels individually, seeing the expanded power they bring, and understanding that each incorporates the previous levels. Normal speakers—adults or children—use these expressive language tools cumulatively.

Gesture - Babies who are no longer hungry clamp their lips. No mistaking that message. A happy baby smiles. People cluster around—gurgling and cooing—trying to coax a repeat. Message received. A defiant two-year-old stamps her foot. Situation clear. If a child hangs his head in remorse, everyone understands, and, with any luck, tries to assuage the guilt. When a weary parent gives a shrug of the shoulder, we know it hasn't been a great day. When someone winks at us across the room, we know we look terrific. When a New York cab driver flips the bird, we know we're in for some shoe-leather time. Gesture, from infant smile all through the most complex layers of Body English, is expressive language without words. Often, when we want to underscore important verbal statements, we couple them with gestures.

Labels - Words are tools for orderly thought. Children who learn what things are called can organize and stabilize their worlds. In *The Magic Years*, Selma Fraiberg gives the example of the baby who, having been put to bed, coos, "Mama, Mama." There is no whine, no petulance, no demand. The child has simply discovered how to invoke that vital person through naming.

As we saw in Chapter One, young children learn new words at the rate of roughly ten per day. The acquisition of labels, which requires patient help from the adult world, allows children to become curators of their personal museums of things,

10 words per day

cataloguing

emotions, ideas, and people. Without words, they cannot catalogue. Without catalogues, there is chaos.

Young children learn our labels and also invent their own.
Three-year-old Amy, with a nearly invisible scratch on her fin-
ger, pointed to the fat pad of her thumb, saying, "Here...on my
thumb-stomach." Arnold, seeing a moustache for the first time,
called it "a *mouth-eyebrow.*" Children not only label in their
own way, they define according to experiences.

The nursery school teacher in our school was having a house
built for her and her husband. Wanting to share the experience
with her young students, she let them build model houses with
blocks, and she drew pictures for them on the blackboard of
each day's new progress. The children learned about foundations, framing, and septic systems. Then, it was time for the
electrician.

"Does anyone know what an electrician does?" she asked.
Tony answered, "He makes wires."
"Good, Tony. He puts the wires in place, so the electricity
can work."
The next week, she asked, "Does anyone know what the
plumber does?"
Amanda volunteered, "He plums."
"Nice idea, Amanda, he puts down the pipes so we can have
water."

Toward the end of the week, she said, "Today, the
sheetrockers are coming. Does anyone know what a
sheetrocker does?"

Jamar said, "I know. He puts sheets on your bed, and then he rocks you to sleep."

Though this definition isn't in the dictionary, its linguistic logic makes it a highly intelligent error. We need to worry when children disconnect words from meaning: "take the *ball* by the horns." A *handburger* can be something you eat with your hands, and *skin milk* at least comes from a cow, but balls don't have horns. Kids who can't tell the meaningful from the nonsensical get "lost in the *shovel.*"

Two Words - If language required a separate label for each event, person, or place, humans would have more memory problems than we already do. Efficiently instead, children learn how to pair a noun with a verb (*Mommy go*), and a label with an adjective (*red ball*) or salutation (*Hi, kitty*). This capacity is usually in place by the time the child is two. And, people of all ages keep right on pairing.

When our grandchildren visit in the summer, they know that while I am sitting on the porch with my breakfast tea and newspaper, I'm "not quite ready for visitors yet." When Willa was three and learning a million new things each day, I would say to her, "Willa, you are some amazing woman!" She would reply, "Granny, I'm not a woman, I'm a girl!" One morning, she wanted to give me a picture she had made. Reading the paper in my wicker rocking chair, I could sense a pair of eyes boring through the newsprint, I could hear heavy breathing, I could see two small, sandy feet. I knew that she knew that I knew she was there, but I didn't say anything. Finally, she erupted, "YO! Woman!"

Children need models for connecting words. They need to *hear* combinations before they can *make* them.

Morphology - Most children, at home and at school, have a workable supply of gestures, labels, and capacities for combination. Morphology lifts language to powerful levels and is usually well-established by the end of kindergarten. Deriving from the Greek *morphe* (form) and *logie* (the study of), the term describes word forms:

morphology ?!

- Pronouns are substitutes for nouns, referring to people or things.

- Plurals change one to many: *cat/cats* or *mouse/mice.*

- The ending *er* changes the form of the word from object to agent: *paint/painter.* Endings of degree create the word forms for size and space: *big/bigger/biggest* or *far/farther/farthest.* These—the language of spatial organization—are building blocks of mathematical understanding. Without these sound bites, children can see spatial organization but neither describe nor command it.

- Verb tenses allow people to arrange their ideas, emotions, and experiences in sequence. Thus filed, they are easy to retrieve for thought or discourse. By adding *s, ing,* or *ed,* the speaker establishes when something happened: *land, lands, landing, landed.* The child who misses these temporal endings fails to acquire an important tool for orderly filing and efficient retrieval.

Irregular plurals and verb tenses are windows to speakers' comprehension. *Mouses* shows understanding of the difference between one or many. "I *branged*" is a brilliant error. If such errors persist beyond kindergarten, however, it is wise to investigate the models from whom the child is receiving language, and to listen for other errors to identify patterns which need attention and correction.

Syntax governs the order of words in sentences, and gives us the structures to create such expressions as declarative sentences (*The girl sat down.*), sentences with dependent clauses (*The girl, who was tired, sat down.*), and questions (*Will the girl sit down?*).

Semantics, sometimes called "pragmatics," is the glue that holds utterances together in meaning. Growing children discover that single words can have multiple meanings. Nine-year-old Arnold passed the collection plate on one side of the aisle in church. Wanting to help God as much as possible, he kept a running calculation as the plate filled. Returning to his pew, he said to his Grandmother, "Wow. I made a bundle!" His five-year-old sister said, "Nuh uh, it's on the washer." *Make a bundle* can either refer to financial wizardry or a collection of dirty laundry.

In most kids, both strands of language follow human inclination, developing normally and robustly. But, in cases of underexposure or discouragement, language does not flourish. It's never too late to repair damage, but it's never too soon to notice gaps and help fill them in. Language proficiency launches or limits academic success and emotional growth.

There are, too, some children whose language systems are innately weak. All of them need recognition, many of them need generalized help, and some need formal diagnosis and specific therapy. Otherwise, they face increasing difficulty and discouragement as they go through school. These kids have trouble with the "4 R's"—*recognition, rate, retrieval,* and *relevance.*

Recognition - Some kids of average or greater than average intelligence have trouble remembering letter names and sounds. They need multi-sensory teaching which incorporates visual, auditory, and kinesthetic/tactile pathways to soak letters with such strong connotation that they become memorable.

Rate - Some people pick their words with great care, valuing both precision and nuance, and may pause searching for just the right word. That's fine.

How about volume? Nowhere is it written that intelligent communication has to be lengthy. Although pithy is pungent, some teachers and parents continue to think a long paper is better than a short one. We need to remember the Gettysburg Address, and also the college senior who handed in his term paper, saying, "If I'd had more time, I could have made it shorter."

Retrieval - Some people have trouble remembering specific labels. Anyone who constantly uses such imprecisions as "Hand me the *thingy*," is telling us he's struggling. The shopper who says, "I, um, went to the, um, grocery store. They had some, um, well...really fragrant, I mean fresh, you know, um, native, um, like local produce, oh, cherry tomatoes..." is showing awkward, unreliable retrieval skills. It's not bad attitude, just a weak system. The struggle to remember precise labels slows the rate of speech, not to mention the listener's attention.

weak retrieval system

23

This difficulty has a name: *dysnomia*. *Dys* means difficulty, *nomen* is the Latin word, to name. Thus, dysnomia means trouble with naming. It may also be called *aphasia*: from the Greek *a* (absence of or trouble with) and *phatos* (to speak). Why does it matter?

In addition to disrupting the easy flow of conversation, dysnomia disrupts writing assignments—particularly when time exerts pressure, as during tests and exams. It also slows reading. How?

Reading is a highly integrative task in which we use our eyes, ears, muscles, and internal language to match the meaning we are absorbing with the markings on the page. Proficient readers sense the writer's intent and cast a "linguistic shadow" to foretell what's coming. This requires ready access to deep reservoirs of internal language. When that access is halting, hesitant, or delayed, the rhythm of the reading—and often comprehension—are destroyed.

Here is an interesting distinction. The child who confuses the shapes and constructions of words may see the word *horse* and say *house*. The reader with retrieval problems may see the word *horse* and know it refers to a four-legged creature that walks, trots, canters, and has a mane and tail; but, in trying to retrieve the label, the reader catches a related word instead and says *pony*. *Horse/pony* errors tell us what is misfiring in the reading process.

One guru of the Whole-Language-or-Bust camp says, "Reading is a psycholinguistic guessing game," and such errors don't matter. However, blasting me in a professional journal, he

retrieval problems

24

wrote, "Vail's comments are *bazaar.*" *Bazaar?* Of course. That's where pickpockets forage and dross masquerades as gold. Accuracy matters. Dysnomia disrupts it. And, kids who struggle need help.

Relevance - Kids need to organize themselves in time and space, by filing and sorting who did what to whom and when. They need to be intimately familiar with the 6 *wh* comprehension words (*who, what, when, where, why, how*) singly and in a group, using them as an organizational grid. Kids with spongy organization ramble, bring in extraneous information, put vital concepts in obscure places, and miss the mark. Organizing, as we see in more detail in Chapter 10, is one of the prime functions of language.

Receptive and expressive language strands compose the heard, spoken, read, and written symbol system which is our deeply needed—and seriously jeopardized—passepartout.

"key of universal access"

So what are we supposed to do about all this?

1. Heighten our own awareness of why language matters, how its two strands work together, and what happens if one or both is weak.

2. Pay attention to spontaneous speech. Kids' words tell us what they think they've heard. When the music from the cassette player went dead, sixth grade Timothy said, "Just turn up the *valium.*"

3. Notice the presence or absence of word endings. Kids who have not taken them in receptively won't use them in spontaneous speech. If they don't use them in speech, they certainly

ending markers

won't use them in writing. What will they do when they meet them in reading? SKIP. Kids who skip over markers of time or space in their reading suffer dreadful comprehension consequences.

4. Note the accuracy and precision of kids' questions and answers. A child with language difficulty may answer, *"Fine,"* when asked, "How old are you?"

5. Listen to the music, rhythm, and melody of kids' speech, noticing monotone or chop, and then making sure such kids are exposed to finer linguistic offerings.

6. Model correct language, so our children receive correct impressions. When they make mistakes, we need to translate the incorrect to the correct, and return it without criticism. For example, Johnny said, "I already *eatened* it." His Mother said, "Oh, you've already eaten it? I bet it was good."

7. Read aloud to our children, laying down deep and rewarding language experiences which will summon them to return. If the realities of life prevent a story hour—a *reading* time—we need to share the experience of listening together to books or stories on tape, saving time to discuss them later.

8. Budget time for conversation with our children.

9. In school, arrange small groups *hetero*geneously; be amazed at the results.

10. In school, arrange small groups *homo*geneously; be amazed at the results.

Three Circles

Intellectual Development, Social/Emotional Development, and Language Development

A s the illustrations indicate, these three circles overlap, such that damage to one will hurt the others. Each depends on the others' intactness, fullness, and integrity.

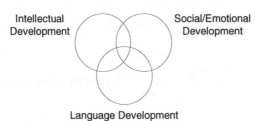

What do we hope to see? What are trouble signs?

Intellectual Development

Potential gifts and talents lie within each of us at birth. They are the mysteries we hope to disclose to ourselves, and which we invite the world to discover in us. We are not talking here about percentiles or stanines on standardized test scores, or of single-number IQ scores. Instead, we are looking at the unfolding of intellect, general milestones, common expectations, tools for learning, and conceptual growth. Far from being limited to achievement levels in school, we know that intellectual power can either accompany academic success, or flower in extra-curricular fields. Here are six trustworthy guides.

1. In his barrier-breaking book, *Frames of Mind: the Theory of Multiple Intelligences,* Howard Gardner points out that humans have at least seven discrete intelligences, only two of which help kids get on the honor roll. The other five are thought of in most schools as pleasant extras. The first two are logical/mathematical and linguistic intelligences. The next five are musical, spatial, bodily-kinesthetic, interpersonal, and intrapersonal. Looking at this list we see how many contributions to civilization come from the five "extras." Looking for potential gifts or talents in our students or offspring, we need to remember Gardner's list.

Language underlies and over-arches these intelligences. The links from language to mathematical, linguistic, interpersonal, and intrapersonal intelligences are so obvious it would be insulting to the reader's intelligence to expand on them. As to the other three, music is a language of its own, and one which often joins with lyrics in mutually supporting ways. Spatial and bodily/kinesthetic intelligences, whose expressions do not depend on words, nevertheless are often paired with language. And, as we will see frequently throughout the book, gesture and Body English are powerful expressive tools.

2. Alan and Nadine Kaufman are the authors of a test called the Kaufman Assessment Battery for Children (K-ABC). They continue the work of the Russian neurologist, A.R. Luria, distinguishing between *sequential* and *simultaneous* processing. In the former, learners collect little bits of information which they systematically build up into concepts or information. This linear, orderly approach matches the design of most textbooks and fits well with many adults' teaching styles. However, it is not Holy Writ.

Simultaneous processing is more global or holistic. Kids who learn this way need to have an overview of the whole concept, which they can then break down into small increments and reassemble. If they try or are forced in school to build concepts from the ground up—sequentially—they misplace the bits of information along the way or simply don't know what to do with them.

This distinction is worth mentioning because roughly 80% of commercially available educational materials are written by sequential processors for kindred spirits. Others must fend for themselves. Many kids with extraordinarily high potential are simultaneous processors who, ironically, are low achievers in school. Leaving them misunderstood—struggling with irritating and confusing methods and materials—is like leaving a tinder box under a magnifying glass in the sun.

3. Joseph Renzulli, champion and protector of the gifted, uses a three-circle model to depict his population. The area of overlap is where he expects to find realized potential.

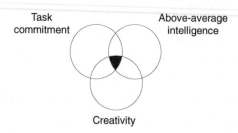

We need to notice that he puts no numerical ceiling on above-average intelligence. Task commitment on the part of the learner requires that teachers provide opportunities for students to explore and showcases for their discoveries. Creativity, like tact or humor, cannot be taught but can be unlocked. Glimmers can grow bright with encouragement.

Where does language figure in? Language and intelligence are mutually supportive. Task commitment expands through words of constructive criticism, encouragement, questioning, or praise. And, language is often the medium for expressions of creativity.

4. Albert Galaburda, continuing the explorations of the late Norman Geschwind, explains that some people (perhaps 25-30% of the overall population) arrive in the world with brains organized for high potential in such three-dimensional realms as engineering (which includes being able to fix the family car), science, medicine, mathematics, athletics, drama, the arts, or politics. This positive potential on the one hand brings nega-

tive factors on the other: high risk for two-dimensional, abstract, symbolic work. In Galaburda's words, these people come with a neuronally ordained "climate inhospitable to language."

These kids show wide discrepancies in their strengths and weaknesses: the nimble-witted math buff who is a reluctant, halting reader, the beautifully coordinated athlete with illegible handwriting, the person who makes wonderful contributions to verbal discussions but can't get thoughts down on paper, or the person who can't channel and focus an explosion of good ideas. Intellectual development will be ragged for these people, as they soar in their spatial realms and struggle with their reading, writing, and pencil-paper arithmetic.

5. In my own work with the gifted, I have collected ten traits which frequently cluster together: instant recognition of concepts, awareness of patterns, empathy, drive, curiosity, energy (psychological and intellectual, as well as physical), powerful concentration, heightened perceptions, divergent thinking, and extensive memory. These capacities—both bane and blessing—nourish intellectual development just as certainly as they cause trouble in some school settings.

All ten depend on and harness language. Underdeveloped or inaccurate language bottles up expression and prevents smooth explanation. These, in turn, lead to frustration and irritation.

6. Theodore Sizer urges us to look for such habits of mind as diligence, persistence, curiosity, willingness to follow through, and the ability to use constructive criticism. According to Sizer and others at The Coalition of Essential Schools, the emer-

gence of these habits—not the completion of Carnegie units—distinguishes the lifelong learner.

Sizer pays particular attention to the term *discourse*, by which he refers to a person's ability to absorb information, form an opinion, explain an idea, listen to other points of view; then to either defend the original opinion, modify it, or throw it out and start over. This high-level use of vocabulary, organization, and establishment of hierarchies and priorities is virtually impossible without strong verbal equipment.

These six models help us interpret the interface of intellectual development and language.

Now, let's consider five aspects of intellectual development which underlie academic power.

- Abstract concept development requires words.
- Memorization—rote or for reason—requires words.
- Making connections and drawing parallels requires words.
- Organizing intellectual intake and output requires words.
- Planning requires words.

What happens when—to paraphrase the old saying—the intellect is willing but the language is weak?

- When language and print don't relate, learning stalls. The newspaper reader who misreads *ballet* for *battle* delivers leaps and pirouettes instead of guns and mortars.

- When language doesn't have roots, concepts collapse. The reluctant reader, who wanted to sound fancy on a college application, wrote of a character in a Greek play, "This hero suffered from an *edible* complex."

o—r When language doesn't grow, children are limited to one meaning per word. Third grade Kenneth suddenly started having trouble in math. Puzzled, I went to observe and found the group doing conversion exercises: inches to feet, feet to yards, etc. After using manipulatives, the teacher said, "Now turn to page 37 in your book and use the table to do the rest of the problems." Kenneth opened his book, collected twelve rulers and tried to fit them on the table.

I said, "Help yourself out; you can use the table."

"I am," he said.

I pointed to the shaded part of the page. "Do you know what this is?"

"A chart or something, I guess."

"It's called a table. You can use it to do all the problems without having to fool around with rulers and yardsticks."

"Table? Are you kidding? I thought a table was furniture."

None of the other kids laughed, because Kenneth, the star hockey player, was a cool kid; the night before he had scored a hat trick against the Bedford Bears.

o—r When language doesn't connect, kids can't branch out. Low-language kids may learn to read individual words and even answer simple factual questions: *What color was Ted's car?* These same kids hit brick walls when asked to use inference: *Why didn't Ted go home?* Inference, along with other higher order reading comprehension skills, makes complex material comprehensible.

Third grade is a watershed year for this. Kids move from learning to read to reading to learn. Neurologically, a big

3rd!?
not 4th

switch takes place: early reading is pattern recognition, later reading (which starts in third grade) is language recognition. These two functions, lodged in different parts of the brain, are both necessary for a smooth journey along the reading continuum.

Third graders with weak language, who have happily memorized their arithmetic combinations, stall out on word problems.

o— When language doesn't expand, children can't shift rhythms, activities, or lexicons as they try to manage smooth transitions.

Activities have different rhythms: "If we hurry along now, we can relax when we get to the beach." It's not just kids. Adults, too, appreciate warnings: "I'll pick you up in twenty minutes." Those whose language has not expanded to include such organizing words as *later, until, before, whenever,* or *under no circumstances* don't have the verbal tools to wind down, phase out, or gear up.

Academic subjects have individual lexicons: "Which number is the *subtrahend?*" "*Primogeniture* governed the transfer of property." "Underline the *predicate.*" "Move your *mouse.*" "*Stage left.*" "What *symmetry.*" "*Half note.*" "Use an *inclined plane.*" Adults whose home lives, work lives, and recreational lives are integrated forget the linguistic shifts kids have to make as they move from one subject to another during a school day. Kids who have trouble remembering labels, learning new vocabulary, or jumping from one lexicon to another end up either overwhelmed or under-educated. Ideally, transitions help kids close the file on one set of ideas, open the file on what's to come, and even take a breath in between.

☛ When language doesn't flow, discourse jolts. Ponderous speakers or inefficient word searchers (remember our friend who bought cherry tomatoes at the market) stupefy their listeners. People who blurt and compress their words are hard to follow.

Those whose handwriting doesn't keep pace with their ideas—in what the neurologists call "kinetic melody"—do poorly on written assignments. They either deliver factory outlet ideas to get rid of the task or dress their good ideas in ragged layout. Papers which appear to represent marginal thought may be graded accordingly.

handwriting

☛ When language is too frail to marshall thoughts, words wander, ideas circle, concepts collide, facts shuffle, and information dissipates. What should be a dress parade turns "to the wind's march."

Social/Emotional Development

To journey from dependence to autonomy, the child must establish a sense of self as separate from others. This distinction between *I* and *you*, big news to the infant, opens the way to *mine* and *yours*—thus, the beginning of conscience. Children need a strong relationship with a caregiving adult to connect, to experience what feels good, and then to return the affection with such baby-generosities as smiles and coos.

Erik Erikson teaches us that children grow through a preordained series of conflicts between opposing emotions such as *trust* vs. *mistrust.* As the child resolves the conflict, he or she is left with what Erikson calls a *positive* or *negative* ratio. This ratio predisposes the positive or negative outcome of the next conflict. Central to this process is the concept of cause and effect, which, in turn, is most often expressed through language. Not limiting himself to children, Erikson explores the classic progression of conflicts from birth to old age:

- Trust vs. Mistrust
- Autonomy vs. Shame and Doubt
- Initiative vs. Guilt
- Industry vs. Inferiority
- Identity vs. Identity Confusion
- Intimacy vs. Isolation
- Generativity vs. Stagnation
- Integrity vs. Despair.[2]

With luck and some love from the world, humans move from self-awareness to self-acceptance, all the while using language to build connections with others. People connect with parents, peers, older and younger kids, strangers, fictional characters, authority figures, lovers, minions, bosses, and creatures of their own imaginings. Weaving with color, texture, and pattern, we shuttle back and forth on the loom of experience, binding together the warp and woof of emotion and connection.

As we explored in *Emotion: The On/Off Switch for Learning,* the limbic system—the emotional brain—has the power either to open or close pathways, doorways, or windows to learning. It is the job of the limbic system to interpret the emotional content of incoming stimuli and then to broadcast that inter-pretation to the entire organism. The limbic system, operating below a conscious level, may say that a sound is neutral, that a person is threatening, or a that a prospect is exhilarating. When the message is neutral, current flows evenly between percep-tion, emotion, and thought. For example, as I am writing this, I can hear the sound of a jackhammer down the street. I recog-nize it, but it is neutral, a non-event.

A negative message shuts down power and breaks connec-tions. Anger, fear, rejection, frustration, and prospects of failure or humiliation—all prompt the limbic system to broadcast an alarm. What happens to language in such circumstances? The person becomes cut off from access to memory, the ability to reason, the ability to make novel connections, the ability to organize thought. These, of course, are closely interwoven with the whole language system.

A positive message opens lines, increases flow, and channels juice. Open circuits and flowing energy bring light to learning. The intellectual, language, and social/emotional circles rein-force as they connect.

Additionally, particular learning styles create specific social/emotional needs. For example, those children with extra intel-lectual dimensions, gifts, or talents need to be more than window dressing for a school catalogue or family picture. They have needs connected to their prowess:

➤ the need to be seen as a child first, and a child with high potential second, o— the need to belong,

o— the need to be a giver as well as a receiver of care,

o— the need to escape the confinement of previous perfection and high performance,

o— the need to share,

o— the need to feel proud,

o— the need to showcase talent and demonstrate mastery without embarrassment,

o— the need to be a student being taught, not a teacher's aide,

o— the need to do the family chores just like everyone else.

In children whose needs are met, the circles plump each other up and out. When needs are neglected, the circles shrivel.

Children with such hampering conditions as <u>the</u> dyslexia<u>s</u> also have particular social/emotional needs. Self-acceptance, self-reliance, and successful strategies will pave the way for deservedly strong self-concept. We know that true sense of worth grows from the inside out. Self-esteem grows from achievement, which is the outgrowth of motivation, which springs from tastes of competence. Confidence is the flower of competence.

Children in the average band need to be nurtured, too, not to be taken for granted. They should not be left to their own devices simply because they don't make trouble. Repaying cooperation with neglect is unfair.

Whatever the child's particular proclivities, social/emotional development overlaps and intersects with language in the following ways:

➤ The baby begins communicating first with fixed gaze, then with smiles and coos, then words, words, words.

➤ Toddlers establish boundaries and learn limits through words that include "Good!" and "No!"

➤ Preschoolers catalogue their worlds by finding out the names for things: "What's this?" They drive their parents nuts, but the results are worth the trouble.

➤ Preschoolers and nursery schoolers make jokes with word play; they consolidate their inner language and acquire social vocabulary which directs interpersonal behaviors...most of the time.

➤ Kindergartners use words to share, take turns, hear stories, tell stories, and laugh superciliously at such wicked creatures as Curious George.

➤ First and second graders use words to explain, listen and empathize. Sam said to George, "Mrs. Smith said your grandmother died. So did my hamster. It's really sad." (That I myself am a grandmother gives me permission to tell that story. It's hard to imagine a higher compliment.)

➤ Third graders use words to bargain, to be cool, and to make friends in a new way: slinging gleeful insults and making puns. Pity the kid who can't join the repartee. What's the alternative? Revert to baby talk, become the class clown, and if you can't talk fast, burp fast.

◦━ Fourth graders through law school students, and those on into the upper reaches of old age, use words to trade physical assault for verbal bargaining. They establish rules for games and argue loudly about changing or bending them. They use words to make friends, express disappointment, challenge loyalty, extend friendship, question procedures, or propose marriage.

◦━ Throughout life, through language, each of us is the central character in the drama of our lives.

When language goes awry, social/emotional development suffers. Kids who lack the language for taking turns make enemies instead of friends. Weak language prevents sharing feelings, trading news, making plans. Kids who process language slowly may not hear or catch on to the new rules for the game, becoming pariahs in the process. It takes language to infer the acceptable code of group behavior and to conform one's own behavior to it. Kids who can't do that make themselves outcasts. Adolescents who lack the language to keep up seek maladaptive alternatives: anti-social outlets for frustration, immediate gratification, and mind-numbing pain killers.

Language Development

Everything in this chapter relates to language development. But, since it is one of the three circles, we should summarize some key points here, running the risk of repetition.

◦━ The central language jobs of the infant, toddler and preschooler are to use and exercise receptive and expressive language strands, letting each strengthen the other.

o— Kindergartners share observations, put sensory experiences and emotions into words, and break words apart into smaller segments, rearranging them in new combinations. They practice wordplay.

o— The language task for first graders is to "take it up and put it down." They take up word recognition and the use of letter sounds for decoding. They put it down by writing their thoughts on paper.

o— Second graders absorb facts, like to learn new terms, and explode with laughter at the foolishness of Amelia Bedelia.

o— Third graders cross the Rubicon mentioned earlier, moving from fact retrieval to inference, to secret clubs with passwords, and to the beginnings of organization by the 6 *wh* words, by sequence, and by categories.

o— Fourth graders, aspiring to easy rhythm between their intake, filing, retrieval, and output, hone their abilities to compartmentalize.

o— Fifth graders (and on up) can hold conflicting points of view, comparing and contrasting, as we will see in greater detail in Chapter 7.

So what are we supposed to do about all this?

1. Encourage children to play with language as they play with Legos: messing with words, inventing new ones, making up crazy combinations (invent a new fruit: *ras-app-a-melon*), rhyming, and taking words apart and putting them back together. This goes by the ten-dollar name of "auditory segmentation" but is nothing more than extracting and rear-

ranging sounds within words. Can you say *rainbow*, and then say it again but leave out *bow*? And, we mustn't stop offering these activities just because people have finished kindergarten. What do poets do?

2. Play with figures of speech, illustrate proverbs, invent new similes.

3. Find ways to showcase talent. Remember Gardner's intelligences and Renzulli's circles.

4. To establish and strengthen connections, read and discuss fairy tales: what are the elements? How are Snow White, Cinderella, and The Wizard of Oz alike? Search for common patterns, for what Henry James called "the figure in the carpet."

5. Teach kids to use Adjust-a-Speak, tailoring their words to fit—variously—peers, authority figures, parents, strangers, teachers, grandparents, younger children, older kids. We can try using a simple sentence (*Will you play with me?*) and saying it in different ways depending on the audience. In addition to slang and kidspeak, students deserve to know the language of formality and manners. This doesn't mean we're going to put them in white gloves and seat them endlessly in drawing rooms. But, manners need not be restrictive. Manners give a shy person a way to reach out to others.

6. On a poster board, write math process signs and vocabulary in color code. Use green, as in growth, for those indicating increase: +, ×, *product, sum, total,* etc. Use red, as in stop, for those indicating shrinkage: −, ÷, *left over, remaining,* etc. Use blue for ratios and equations: =, :, ::, /. Visual cues are strong reminders.

7. Screen for Specific Language Disability, using an individually administered instrument. This can be done by a learning specialist, psychologist, or teacher trained for the purpose. This exercise will pick out those kids whose language is not strong enough to serve them well. We need to screen *all* children; otherwise, the quiet, friendly, drifty but obedient ones—often little girls—are presumed to be just fine. See the Resource Section for reliable titles.

8. Teach kids how to use materials backwards and inside out as well as straight on; read the questions before the selection in a reading comprehension passage, read the conclusion and introduction before reading the content of a textbook chapter. Techniques such as these are very helpful to simultaneous processors.

9. Use word segmentation techniques consistently and all the way through the grades. In the 1970's, Bryant and Bradley did a study. They took groups of kids—similar in background and intelligence—entering school for the first time. Throughout the year, Group One sorted picture cards first by initial sound, then final, then middle sounds. Group Two sorted the cards by such categories as toys and vegetables. Group Three didn't work with the cards at all. By the end of fourth grade, Group One was still far ahead of the others in reading. This replicable study, cited often at Orton Dyslexia Society conferences, shows the same results year after year. The exercises offered in Rosner's book, listed in the Resource Section, are suitable for kids up through sixth grade and beyond. Kids enjoy them.

10. Teach jokes.

Four Manifestations
Listening, Speaking, Reading, and Writing

O ne key, two strands, and three circles lead us to four manifestations. These, standing distinct, are like the "net of gems; where in every gem of the net all others are reflected."

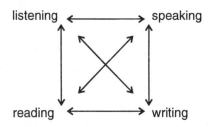

Listening and speaking are horizontal pairs, because they are opposites, as are reading and writing. Vertically, listening and reading go together because they are both receptive. Speaking and writing are the expressive duo. Or, we could make diagonal pairs: writing and listening, as well as reading and speaking, have chicken/egg relationships.

These four are language in space and time. Reading and writing are language laid out in space, always there for retrieval or review. Listening and speaking are language laid out in time. They hang in the air for a second, then vanish.

What do we know about these manifestations, what should we try to discover, how should we encourage robust development?

Listening

"School is a listening place, and I'm a lousy listener," sixth grade Ted said sadly.

If we ask teachers and parents their prime complaint (Adjust-a-Speak: *worry*) about kids today, they say, "They don't know how to listen." If we ask kids their prime problem with adults, they say, "They never listen!"

What's wrong? Is it more than the pernicious effect of TV, which has trained our kids to accompany rapid-fire, jackhammer words with visual images? Can we overcome the effects of that habitual white noise that non-listening people engage in when they use radio sounds to deaden thought and pass time? Can we improve? Of course. Of course. Of course.

First we need to understand what listening requires, then see what kinds of listening skills people need, and then concentrate on making listening appetizing, worthwhile, active, and part of a big purpose.

Listening requires a capacity for hearing. As we will see in Chapter 6, the silent crippler of reduced hearing is increasingly common and frequently undetected. Before we harangue children about their listening, we need to find out how well they hear.

In addition to hearing, listening requires accurate perception of sounds within words, of single words, and of words in context and volume. One of the star inventor/engineers for the country's largest airplane manufacturer said to his wife, "I don't think I'll ever learn to spell."

She said, "That's O.K. I'll help you."

He confessed, "You know what one of my hardest words is? *Tomorrow.* (His pronunciation makes it sound like *ta-ma-ral.*) I know it has an *a* and some *l*'s, but I can't remember where they go."

The browser who says, "Can I see the *mazagine?*" the bed maker who says, "*sleeps* and pillowcases;" or the radio listener who sees mental images of primates on hearing, "*Guerrillas* attacked military strongholds this morning..." are telling us that words they have "heard" aren't the same as the ones that were written or spoken.

Listening also requires memory. Lucky people are born with a metaphoric tape recorder which has excellent fidelity and volume control, both FF and REW buttons, and a nice long tape. These fortunate souls record what they'll need to retrieve, and can replay on demand. Others, however, equally bright, have crackly fidelity, a temperamental volume control, unreliable FF and REW, and a short tape. It's not bad attitude; it's a short tape. But, weak auditory memory sabotages learners in school and out in the world beyond.

Because listening is a receptive activity and generally a quiet behavior, some people count it as passive. True listening is active, aggressive, and imaginative, involving the listener's previous knowledge, reason, emotion, and anticipation. It also takes different forms.

Humans engage in three different kinds of listening. To give ourselves a structure, we might call them *Intensive*, *Extensive*, and *Pensive*. Each makes different demands, promises different rewards, and, of course, in specific situations, people use different combinations.

Intensive listening is what we use for instructions, directions, and facts. "Please take out your yellow book, four markers, an eraser, and your scissors. Open the book to page 24, and do the first three items. When you are through, get the tracing paper." "Go on Route 172 to the gas station. Turn left at the blinker, go 1/2 mile until you pass a graveyard, and a school on the right. When you come to the Y, bear right, sort of, go up the hill and ..." My tape ran out long ago. "12,000 citizens, comprising 67% of the 1994 tax base, voted yesterday to approve a bond issue of two million dollars to be used in the construction of a sewer line, nine miles long, connecting the towns of ..."

This listening offers information and demands fully focused attention and strong memory skills. Like a sprint in running or swimming, it cannot be sustained over a long period. Three strategies help improve Intensive listening:

- repeat the directions to yourself,
- make a mental movie,
- jot down reminders.

Extensive listening helps us select what we want from voluminous incoming information. To do this, we need to know what we're interested in, what we need, what we're searching for, what we already know. We need a grid on which to sort intake.

For example, if I want an up-to-date weather forecast when I am in my car, I turn on WCBS, because I know they broadcast what they call "Traffic and Weather Together on the Eights." I wait until it's :08, :18, :28, :38..., then switch over from NPR to CBS. While I am waiting, I hear (but don't pay attention to) the sports update, the stock market quotes, and the latest from a street-side emergency. These come in predictable sequence. Then, when I hear the music break indicating my information is coming next, I'm all ears.

The major step for successful Extensive listening is to "activate prior knowledge." This skeleton of what we already know gives an armature on which to hang new information. Like a sculptor, we add on the clay of ideas, concepts, facts, and feelings, modeling them into the muscles, flesh, sinews, cartilage, and skin to make a life-like creation.

Pensive listening deserves to be idiosyncratic and needn't be accurate according to others' definitions. Each one of us would hear a Beethoven Concerto differently.

Knowing the processes of listening, the different types, and some strategies to assist each one helps us decide what kinds of listening activities to engage in ourselves, and which to offer the children in our care.

Reading

I asked five children, "What is reading?"

They answered:

•— "When you have to be quiet."

•— "Going places without leaving the room."

•— "Something you get when your baby teeth fall out."

•— "Something you learn in school."

•— "Something I can't do, so I feel bad."

Five adults, asked the same question, replied:

•— "Access to anything."

•— "Escape."

•— "Learning."

•— "I read the paper or comics or magazines or manuals—I love manuals—but read a book? I get too restless."

•— "Something I fake. I don't know how, and everybody else does. I'll never get a girlfriend."

A 17-year-old non-reader, picked up by the police, said to the social worker, "Why shouldn't I steal or do drugs—nuthin' else for me out there."

The highly integrative activity called reading requires exquisite choreography among the visual, auditory, motor, memory, and language systems. As is true with listening, because most people read sitting down, some people mistakenly think it is passive. However, the word *comprehend* comes from the Latin word *prehendere*, meaning to take up or to seize. Passive seizing is an oxymoron.

Parallel to the types of listening, we could make three categories of reading: *Intensive*, *Extensive*, and *Pensive*. Sometimes, grown-ups forget to describe or teach these distinctions to children, who grow up thinking that all "important" reading has to be done the same way.

Intensive reading is for communications from the Bureau of Motor Vehicles, fine print on insurance policies, questions on job applications, and getting into a new subject. Because it must be meticulous, it therefore is usually slow. Faced with an Intensive reading task, we hope it will be short. If we thought we had to read *Gone With the Wind* with Intensive reading, most of us would flee. Intensity requires trustworthy sound/symbol correspondence: there's a world of difference between *hit* and *pet*. Then, it requires crisp recognition of high-frequency "sight words:" *could* and *cloud* offer different portents.

Extensive reading is for shopping the front page of the newspaper—deciding which articles to read, which to read later, and which (probably with guilt) to skip. Like a hunter/gatherer, the reader's eyes wander unsystematically around the headlines, recognizing words, making associations, and sparking interest. Compelling items pull us in; we read right through to the end. Or, we may meander further among the subheadings, seeking twinges of excitement or collapsing in boredom. College students shop through a Required Reading List the same way. So do catalogue browsers, kids taking survey courses, and people who are bored or who have trouble staying focused on what they are reading.

Extensive reading requires memory (working memory as well as rote): "I read a great story about Alaskan wildlife yesterday." The ability to see associations and make connections informs our choices: "I wonder what the differences are between animals in Antarctica and animals in Alaska." As we bring shards, slivers, and chunks from disparate categories to converging zones of thought, we reach out, take in, evaluate, and anticipate: "I saw a sealskin tapestry in a friend's house...it made me wonder about all the ways hunters use oil, fur, meat, sinews, and teeth...I wonder whether this article about scrimshaw talks about elephants as well as whales...I wonder where I put that story about the Iditerod." To use Extensive reading smoothly, a person must be a *con'tent* reader as well as a *content'* one.

Pensive reading is for immersion. Some people glory in study. To the outside eye, they appear to be working hard; but the job is joy, not labor. Other readers dive deep into fiction or sprinkle themselves with poetry. This kind of reading—hypnotic and frequently sensual—doesn't require nit-picking accuracy, instead evoking imagery, emotional response, curiosity, or humor.

When I am immersed in reading, I hear the music of the words and am just as annoyed at being interrupted in mid-paragraph as I would be by chit-chat breaking into the "Ode to Joy." My husband says, "What's the big deal. Go right back to it." But, I can't. The spell is broken.

What happens when reading doesn't work? What are reading problems, how do people get them, what helps?

Frustration, guilt, anger, avoidance, and denial are five common companions to reading disability. Little kids—longing to please the adults in their lives, as well as themselves—are eager to learn to read. For them, it's like uncovering secrets of the adult world—every child's passion. When they cannot do with effort what others around them are doing with apparent ease, they feel ashamed and cross. Our knowledge of the limbic system, the emotional brain, tells us what happens next. Shutdown.

I was working with a first grader who had made a very respectable beginning in learning to read. One day, we couldn't find the reader she was working in. I suggested a different book, but she looked terrified. I said, "I'll help. You can read this book. You know these words."

"Wait," she said. "Stop. You mean they use the same words in different books?" ·

Kids who slip through and get to middle school still being virtual non-readers bluff and bluster their way with camouflage. Older kids and adults who struggle to or cannot read may experience deep shame, often masked with depression, anti-social behavior, withdrawal, or mind-altering substances.

Reading problems may spring from <u>the</u> dyslexia<u>s</u>, or from being pressed into formal academics prematurely, or from difficulty with attention, or from pinched pedagogy which only uses one method. If a child who has trouble remembering sight

Remember Kirk: "Letters have sounds!"

causes

words has a teacher who relies on "Look/Say," the kid pays the price for the teacher's rigidity. Teachers need to use a variety of techniques. Language is built of both structure and texture. Structure gives reliability and predictability; texture gives music and magic. Readers, all ages, need both.

Whatever the root of the problem, prevention is always easier than remediation. Individually administered screenings, which can be given and interpreted by a trained teacher, highlight those children at risk for reading difficulties. Once identified, these children can use methods and materials designed to prevent "the flowering of the vulnerable agent." If children were given appropriate materials from the start, there would be no need for such programs as Reading Recovery. Waiting until a child "deserves" extra help by having failed darkens an already unnecessarily cloudy picture with negative emotional associations and lost time.

Serious problems jump out at us. Shadow problems may drift in and out, or only appear when the kid is older. The student who has been able to manage simple, straightforward passages or basal readers may have trouble as the reading load increases or moves into increasingly demanding abstraction. Reading under pressure of speed, with fatigue, or after a few beers may be disastrous. Other readers may manage concrete materials, but flounder in figurative language or embedded concepts. A dyslexic, being coached for his Medical Boards, missed the following question: Parents of a ten-year-old diagnosed asthmatic need to be told: a...b...c...d... The student didn't know who had the asthma.

Developmentally appropriate schooling, multi-sensory materials (designed originally for dyslexics but phenomenally successful with all beginning readers), a positive emotional classroom climate, and a solid language base make reading possible for virtually everyone. Taking the mystery away also helps. As the Texan said, "Shucks. Readin' an' writin' ain't nuthin' but talkin' writ down."

Speaking

Describing an old windbag, George Bernard Shaw said, "He has lost the power of conversation, but unfortunately not the power of speech."

Thinking about different reasons to speak, I found thirteen *R* words and two *L*'s. Readers will think of others.

1. *Request:* "Please pass the salt."

2. *Require:* "You must wear shoes to dinner."

3. *Relate:* "You'll never guess what she did then!"

4. *Refuse:* "No, thank you, I already have a blueberry muffin."

5. *Repeat:* "Remember what Abraham Lincoln said in the Gettysburg Address..."

6. *Relinquish:* "Now I understand why you want it so badly. Here. Take it with my blessing."

7. *Regurgitate:* "On this test, I will list four reasons for war which you wrote on the board."

8. *Rehash:* "I know you said you were sorry, but I don't think you realize what you said."

9. *Reward:* "Your first rate performance earns you a 75% raise."

10. *Ramble:* "Well, well. I'll just chat along. Silence is so empty."

11. *Ridicule:* "You're wearing THAT?"

12. *Rule:* "Having seized the radio station, I will now give orders to the citizenry."

13. *Relish:* "I can't wait to tell you what I've learned!"

1. *Love:* "It is the dawn and Juliet is the sun."

2. *Lies:* "Not me. I swear."

Because we don't want to criticize a child or interrupt expressive flow, the generous-spirited translate from wrong to right. But, we need to stay alert to misarticulations, malapropisms, Spoonerisms, misinterpretation, trumpery, floaters, and out-loud silent speech, because they betray linguistic confusion. Everyone makes occasional errors; frequency and consistent patterns are warning signals.

o—⊤ Slushy pronunciation may result from a mouth full of braces or mentally slippery words: "Many died of *Blue Bonnet* plague."

o—⊤ Malapropisms: "That thief had his hand in the *tiller* all along."

o—⊤ Sounds out of sequence convey unintentional messages, *a la* Spooner: he bought *lemons* instead of *melons*.

o—⊤ Body English is often a tip-off to misinterpretation, particularly of figures of speech: a third grader, waiting for gravity to do her work for her, tipped her head sharply to one side when I said, "Think it *over*."

•— My favorite trumpery is: "How old were you when you were seven?"

•— Floaters are words disconnected from meaning: the fifth grader (who had just played the role of Mary in the Christmas Pageant) was learning how to lay out a final draft in English class. Excitedly, she pointed to the red vertical line on the left-hand side of her paper and volunteered, "You should always keep a tidy *virgin* on the side."

•— Out-loud silent speech results when people use words they have seen but not heard. I was a freshman in college before I discovered that the word *awry* doesn't rhyme with *glory*. It was then I also learned the proper pronunciation of *bedraggled*, which to me had always been *bed-raggled*.

Many kids, particularly those unaccustomed to conversation, need to practice Adjust-a-Speak. Skits are ideal vehicles. Take a simple sentence: "Why can't you come over?" Ask pairs of children to invent a dialogue asking and answering the question optimistically, hospitably, jealously, angrily, or defensively.

Writing

"Written speech is a separate linguistic function, differing from oral speech both in structure and mode of functioning. Even its minimal development requires a high level of abstraction. It is speech in thought and image only, lacking the musical, expressive, intonational qualities of oral speech. In learning to write, the child must disengage himself from the sensory aspect of speech and replace words by images of words..." [1]

Vygotsky, Leo, Thought & Language

hand writing

There are additional hurdles for young writers to clear. We know that some kids avoid writing because their lag-along hands don't keep up with their ideas, making pencil pushing cumbersome. When I had the flu, first grade Chris made me a get-well card. On a heart-shaped paper, he drew a picture of a kid sitting at a desk writing. The bubble said, "I hate this." In another bubble, he drew himself watching TV, saying, "I love this." His message to me was, "If you're sick, you get to watch TV. Don't get well."

organization

Kids feel ashamed when their written work is returned with red markings all over it, and we know that some kids who understand a great deal have trouble getting their ideas down on paper during tests or exams. These kids have trouble with both appearance and organization, a deadly combination. Ward was the top student in his science class, yet his exam was marked *F* with the comment, "I cannot read one word of this handwriting."

Fear of writing vanishes if we see it as a craft, as well as art. William Zinsser, in *On Writing Well,* says the craftsman improves simply by practicing. The same is true of writing. If you want to be a better writer, write. Write daily. Then, read a good writer and write some more.

Good writing need not be florid; neither must it be lengthy. There is Brancusian beauty in a lean, declarative sentence: "I love you." There is safety in a clear note on the refrigerator: "There is enough cold chicken for everybody." There is power in brevity: "Marry me!" There is action in sports writing: "His arm is fast enough to throw a lamb chop past a wolf."

This may be the place to mention that the Writing Process—a philosophical approach to the teaching of writing which burst upon the scene about ten years ago and has attracted passionately loyal adherents—isn't the one and only way to teach writing. Junior high and high school teachers, along with college professors, are telling us that students who have been brought up only on the Writing Process are hooked on "finding their own voices"—spending enormous amounts of time for very small output and having trouble shifting among different kinds of writing. For example, they have trouble with expository prose; producing clear, written summaries; or writing on demand. Students are ill-served by the exclusivity and chauvinism which unfortunately have framed the cultish aspects of a good idea.

To help people of all ages find the "Joy of Lex," we need to banish the evil three: fear, shame, and fatigue. Then, encourage the glorious trio: humor, power, and permanence. How?

To help writers climb over fear, start small. Ask them to use index cards, not big pieces of blank paper. No one is scared of an index card. Set aside time to chart and catalogue ideas. Some will never be used. That's OK. They're captured. Kids get scared when they have to think up an idea and write about it at the same time.

To banish shame, throw away the red pen. Make corrections with pencil marks which the kid can erase when the error is gone. Understand the linguistic roots of errors and NEVER mock. As we have seen over and over, errors betray the language confusions we need to identify. Be grateful for them, and use the knowledge they provide.

┐─ Fourth grade Agatha, learning punctuation marks wrote: "Use the *its-slam-a-shun* point." Suffering from frequent colds, allergies, and ear infections, she never heard the sounds inside *exclamation*. Absent from school, she missed the lesson on *tion*.

┐─ College senior and dyslexic, Maria wrote of seeing a *doctornintry*. She had the courage to try; the word *documentary* was important to her, and her proofreader or spell-checker will bail her out. She also said, "I have *dix-lep-si-um* (dyslexia), but, *thinks* (thank) goodness, they know how to help. I can *sickle orses* (select courses)."

┐─ A third grade teacher, writing a report on a child whose weak memory was holding her back, wrote, "I am teaching Elsie some *pneumonic* devices." I sure hope they pump her up!

┐─ A parent, writing about the importance of being orderly, wrote proudly of his son, "Adam is very *mythodical*." If myth is metaphor, Adam will rest on his laurels.

Issues and errors like these need early attention and recognition. Otherwise, they continue into adulthood, making the writer look foolish.

Fatigue is usually a harvest of poor or insufficient handwriting instruction. And, no, keyboards won't make handwriting obsolete. We need to restore and extend handwriting instruction from K-4 (6 when necessary). This will mean teaching teachers as well as kids; many of them, in relics of '60s fashions, think handwriting instruction inhibits creativity. The opposite is true; it undergirds creativity.

Let's also abandon teaching two manual systems (manuscript and cursive) and settle on one which we will teach, kids will practice, and writers will use.

Why not just rely on electronics? Every kid needs one legible, comfortable, written symbol system: for taking notes in class when the laptop battery dies, for taking phone messages and keeping golf scores, and for writing thank-you letters, love letters, and nail-down-the-job-after-the-interview handwritten letters. To spare kids the nuisance of learning correct handwriting is to deny them a big share of the profits of literacy.

Now, let's encourage the good three: humor, power, and permanence.

↦ Sometimes, teachers and students think that to be "real," writing must be heavy, long, solemn, and didactic. The light touch in the written word is a feather-kiss.

↦ Power in writing comes from emotion, illumination, organization, knowledge to share, sense of purpose and audience, and from rewriting. Distasteful? Not at all. From shooting hoops to turning corners on two wheelers, kids enjoy practicing what they've discovered they're already a little bit good at.

↦ Humans are always hunting around for immortality. The permanence of the written word offers a toe-hold.

So what are we supposed to do about all this?

1. Provide a successful launch, and then encourage children to harness emotions in what they're describing.

2. Let them cast the light of their own perception on the image offered to the reader.

3. Teach them the multitude of ways to organize explained in the titles and materials in the Resource Section.

4. Show them how to find knowledge worth sharing.

5. Let them fashion their work to fit the purpose and audience. Here's another form of Adjust-a-Speak. With these priorities, they will conduct the music of their own writing.

6. Allow time for pretending. There should be no age ceiling on this. Through this noble abstraction, kids practice the thoughts, words, and Body English of other people or species. This is language in practice and flexibility.

7. Decide on one manual symbol system (per school or per student), teach, train, allow time for practice, and showcase!

8. Show teachers how to use the multi-sensory (visual, auditory, kinesthetic, tactile) materials originally designed for those with dyslexia or Specific Language Disability, but suitable and successful for all students. This way, no one slips through the net.

9. Use games to teach quick, accurate recognition of sight words.

10. Make a "Sometimes I Feel..." collection. Using alphabetical order, 26 index cards, and a notebook ring, help each writer make a collection of Sometimes I Feel angry, bossy, careless, devilish, energetic, etc. Use this as a base for writing.

Five Sources
Language Pools, Rivers, Oceans, Lakes, and Springs

Unlike shopping for vine-ripened tomatoes, soft shell crabs, or a becoming bathing suit, we hunt for language unconsciously. Relying on osmosis, we absorb it indiscriminately. Standing in line at the supermarket, reading in the library, eavesdropping on gossip, we soak up the language around us. Some is strong and well-formed, some flabby, and some not worth noting. We absorb first and sort later, hoping to jettison the junk. But, still, we keep useless litter in our minds, just as we do in our desk drawers or pockets, catching ourselves by surprise at remembering the number of our hotel room on a business trip five years ago, or all the words to the Flintstones theme song.

"It is so with words and patterns. They accumulate in layers, and as the layers thicken, they govern all use and appreciation of language thenceforth. Like music, the patterns of melody, rhythm, and quality of voice become templates against which we judge the sweetness and justness of new patterns and rhythms; and the patterns laid down in our memories create expectations and hungers for fulfillment again. It is the same for the bookish person and the illiterate. Each has a mind programmed with language...from prayers, hymns, verses, jokes, patriotic texts, proverbs, folk sayings, cliches, stories, movies, radio, and television.

"I picture each of those layers of experience and language gradually accumulating and thickening to form a kind of living matrix, nourishing like a placenta, serving as a mini-thesaurus or dictionary of quotations, yet more retrievable and interactive and richer because it is so one's own, steeped in emotional colour and personal associations." [1]

Where do these layers come from? I see five main sources from which children draw language: home, friends, media, school, and their own imaginations. Of course, these also run together and flow in confluence.

Home

Family living is the child's first exposure to language, offering up samples of single words, narratives, exchanges, and varied levels of complexity and emotional tone. In addition to "real talk," each family has its own patois. For example, throughout the early years of parenting and even today, when I put a platter of food in front of my husband to serve at the table, he says, "What are the rest of you having?" The children—and now the grandchildren—all groan. Corny, but it's part of our lore.

All families have their own internal language, and many have more than they realize. A boyfriend of one daughter, who had come to spend the weekend, shook his head on Sunday morning, saying, "This whole family speaks in code."

o—⊤ Family life is a pool of the language of ritual: church talk, holiday chatter, wedding sentiments, funeral murmurings. For each, we have what we say, what we sing, and what we write.

o—⊤ Along with ritual, each family has its spoken and unspoken language of taboo: gossip which is allowed, implied, or forbidden. It's OK to joke about Aunt Ella's new hair color, but not about her false leg. The family language of taboo gives every member reminders about behavior. When our kids were growing up, we had what was called the "minimum standard of acceptable behavior"—a formal slogan for setting limits. When someone was starting to get out of line, all my husband or I had to do was start saying, "minimum ..." They knew just what we meant, and could then elect to shape up or be defiant.

o—⊤ Each family's personal code contains the language of slangy affection. Nicknames are a perfect example. Our youngest kid is named Angus. His sisters call him "Ango-Bango" or "Fungus Among Us." One beautiful granddaughter named Willa is called "Willa Gorilla." At home, in school, at work, or anywhere, being given a nickname (even one which sounds like an insult) is a badge of belonging. Outsiders who use nicknames prematurely are either chastised or walled out.

o—⊤ In family life, we share the language of our nuclear (or extended) unit. It's like the old saw about prisoners who—having spent lots of years locked up together—don't bother to re-tell their jokes or frequent sayings. They just call out their numbers.

When the food is bad, one might say, "Fourteen." To which someone in a nearby cell might reply, "Yeah, and eleven, too."

➤ Families have their predictables: "Don't slam the door." Like all others, our family has idiosyncratic languages of household maintenance: "Get squeezies" is shorthand for saying to the person heading out to the grocery store, "Please pick up some toilet paper."

➤ Those of us who have lived together for a long time often talk without using words. My husband and I bought a new telephone answering machine. But, if we are sitting on the porch, the number of rings we have programmed before automatic pickup doesn't give us enough time to go inside, get to the phone, and pick it up. When this happened yesterday, my husband started to say, "We ought to..." and I immediately said, "I will." Annoyed that I responded before he had gotten the words out of his mouth, he petulantly said, "Will what?" I knew what he had been about to say, I knew which words he would choose to say it, and I agreed. Why go through the whole process? (Maybe it's more pleasant?)

How else do we create the pools of language?

➤ We reminisce, finding the glue of shared memories: we use the language of revisiting.

➤ We absorb the language of our neighborhoods and carpools, each with its unique lexicon.

➤ We talk to our pets. Think of the secrets poured into the ears of Spot and Fido. And, it's not only children who revert to baby talk. I heard a cultured, intelligent woman talking to her poodle: "There's my good Fifi. She's saying she wants her nappy nap, but first she has to have her little walk and tinkle. Yes, Fifums, you're my itty bitty boopy doopy love bug." Pet talk gives adults permission to talk to themselves or to talk baby talk without embarrassment.

◦━ Kids use their families to test out their language—to see what goes. The summer our middle daughter was fifteen, she admired a dark-haired, handsome fellow who carried around a copy of *The Dead Souls*, trying to look literary and mysterious. His name was Tyler. Tyler was too young to have a driver's licence, but he had an older friend named Merriman, the coolest dude in the school. Merriman offered to drive Tyler to our house, where they had been invited to spend the night. Tyler sleeping under our roof: too much happiness! Our daughter, who had been fixing and re-fixing the guest room, finally came downstairs. "Dad," she said, "just do me one favor. When Tyler comes downstairs for breakfast, DON'T say 'Good Morning' in that weird way you always do. I'll die if you say 'Good Morning' like that. What would Merriman and Tyler think?"

But, the job of family members is to remain constant, warts and all, providing a stage set against which the adolescent can position various people to see what combinations work. If the family shifts, the kid loses the background.

With so many families dissolving and recombining, many of today's children have blood siblings, half-siblings, step-siblings, ex-step-sibs, parents, step-parents, parents' live-in or live-out boyfriends and girlfriends. Each category has its own set of manners, levels of intimacy, and, therefore, language.

o━ Most importantly, of course, families have the language of genuine affection, support, coaching, mutual involvement, delight in one another's successes, and solace in times of frustration or discouragement.

Friends

Friends share rivers of common interest. From Pleasant Company dolls to Harleys and tattoos, friends trade with each other in the common parlance of the pursuit.

o━ Friends exercise the language of introduction, as they tell one another about other friends or family members.

o━ Friends test each other out with the different languages of different personas, practicing being dedicated Olympic trainees, hairdressers, sculptors, gourmet cooks, teeny bopper Valley girls, or Schwartzenegger look-alikes.

o━ Friends use language to establish the borders of inclusion and exclusion. Secret clubs have passwords. Gossip determines who's cool and whose father says "Good Morning" in a really weird way. Popularity—as different from friendship as a soap bubble is from a diamond—hangs by a linguistic thread. Kids push each other out with the language of being mean. No instruction required.

o━ Kids band together through the language of team play. They egg each other on through the language of plans. They crack each other up with in-jokes. Just as they "hang around" together, they "word around" together.

Media

The media provides oceans of ready-made language. TV brings tidal waves of slogans, sayings, quotes, theme songs, and canned laughter. These engulf kids in the repertoires of sales, stories, sitcoms, adventure, cartoons, rock, rap, and violence.

VCRs and cable TV are bringing back the oldies, and now we have whole new groups of kids discovering "supercala-fragilisticexpealidocious" and "Where's the beef?"

TV and radio each offer the language of narrative, news, lyrics, and learning. TV automatically provides imagery, but kids need to generate their own. It's the key to reading comprehension, not to mention being a joyful mental ramble. We can help them develop their unused imagery muscles by showing a TV program without sound and asking them to tell what happened, giving characters the voices and vocabulary that seem appropriate. We can then have them hear a program without showing them the picture. Can they explain what happened? What did the characters and set look like?

Judging by the increasing popularity of radio theater and such shows as Prairie Home Companion, the human animal craves this kind of activity.

In newspapers and magazines, we find the language of current events, finance, graphs, society, fashion, obituaries, health, science, sports, editorials, and cartoons. Each is as different from the other as a tidal pool is from a tsunami.

School

In school, kids dive into well-delineated, separated lakes of "kid talk" and "teacher talk." Some students, underexposed to language and unpracticed in its production, need to learn how to speak with adults respectfully, politely, and clearly. They need to know how to challenge or disagree without being rude. They need to know how to acknowledge authority without groveling. Since these are skills they will need for successful adulthood, it is not repressive to teach them; it is small-minded to withhold them.

Other kids—often only children, precocious kids, kids who spend more time in books than on playgrounds, or kids who for one reason or another have spent a lot of time with adults—need to learn "kid talk." Without it, they will be isolated. School is the place to soak it up.

↦ Humor is the *lingua franca* of the school kid. Jokes, puns, insults, passwords, and nicknames are the medium of exchange. I would be a fool to say that all juvenile humor is appetizing. But, I will say that humor is a high form of linguistic abstraction. Not counting the pratfall, humor involves seeing a person or situation, defining the central kernel or salient feature, lifting it out, putting a twist on it so it is different but still recognizable, then putting it back and presenting the new creation to the world. To recognize a salient feature, to add a twist, and to reposition requires rapid, skillful language.

↦ In school, kids learn the language of learning: organizing, depicting, challenging, persuading, changing, summarizing, defining, leapfrogging, and, of course, filing and retrieving.

o━ School trains kids in the language of participation: team play, drama groups, yearbook, committees, glee club, or special interest groups.

o━ To write, students need to command the languages of discussion, essay, exposition, narrative, fiction, fact, and humor. Where will these powers come from? Children who have heard and read these genres will be familiar with the tools specific to each one.

Imagination

Language is a wellspring of pretending and—at the same time—a conduit for expression. Mistakenly thought of as appropriate only for young children, pretending is a route to empathy, reading comprehension, writing power, humor, adventure, and identification. Successful make-believe requires a high level of abstraction.

o━ For Thomas to become a lion, for example, he needs to see what it is that makes him a boy, determine the essential nature of "lionhood" (gait, growl, intent, size, demeanor), run a quick compare and contrast, choose what facets of lionhood to adopt, what bits of "personhood" to relinquish, and then go for it. This kind of sorting depends on language, even though it happens rapidly and probably without conscious dips in the springs of language.

o━ Drama is formalized pretending, joining Body English, rehearsed speech, and pretending in one glorious combination. Less formally, role playing helps kids see how others may react to their actions. Both are fun for young children, teenagers, and adults, as pretending itself should be for people of all ages.

internal dialog

◦→ Just as the young child creates inner language, older kids (and adults, too) set up internal dialogue. Internal dialogue lets us be anyone we wish. Haven't we all invented the perfect riposte riding home in the car? Don't we set up conversations in our heads, testing out how to soothe or query or get the upper hand?

Tells why

◦→ In *The Optimistic Child*, Martin E.P. Seligman describes the vital role of "explanatory style" in self-concept. (And, it goes without saying that language is the tool of explanation.) Seligman points out that a positive explanatory style ("I worked hard; I deserved that high grade," or "I need to practice batting. I don't want to keep striking out.") gives children feelings of competence and autonomy. Although things won't always work out perfectly, it helps to lay plans and reach goals.

A negative explanatory style ("No wonder I flunked; that teacher hates me," or "I'll never get a hit; I'm no good.") puts power in the hands of fate, leaving the kid a helpless victim. Positive explanatory style comes from—and builds in—optimism. Negative explanatory style reinforces pessimism and predisposes the child to failure.

How you talk to yourself helps determine who you are. Explanatory styles fuse language, emotion, intellect, and probability.

◦→ Inventions give language free rein. Several years ago, St. Martin's Press published *After Man: A Zoology of the Future*, in which author Dougal Dixon uses genetics and the course of evolution so far to chart and describe the creatures who may be on the planet after humans have vacated. His creatures—reminiscent of Lewis Carroll's "bandersnatch" and "slithy toves," or Edward Lear's *Scroobious Pip*—range from horrendous to adorable.

One needn't be a paleontologist to play the game. For fun, ask each kid in a class or family to invent a never-before animal: give it a name and describe its habitat, its eating preferences, its circadian rhythms, its predators, and its partners. Make an illustration. Introduce the creatures to one another. Which will be friends? Which will kill each other off? Which can be domesticated? There is no limit to the imaginative opportunities.

⊶ Fantasy and imagery are yin and yang. We have the imagery we concoct from hearing words: "to build the trout a crystal stair, to comb the hillside's thick green hair".[2] We have the verbal associations which bubble up from hearing music or seeing a work of art.

⊶ Language and dreams of omnipotence go together. Think of Superman, "who as Clark Kent, a mild-mannered reporter for a major metropolitan daily..." From Mark Twain to Dr. Seuss, writers have launched fantasies of omnipotence from the platform of language.

Refreshing ourselves, navigating, testing our courage or endurance, fishing, diving, or simply listening and watching, we immerse ourselves continually in the pools, rivers, oceans, lakes and springs of language.

So what are we supposed to do about all this?

1. Through reading aloud or through tapes, expose children to the music of poetry.

2. Using the suggestions above—or others which occur to children—help them invent new creatures.

3. Provide cascades of delicious and suitable humor. Laughter is a dowser's wand to the pools of affect, energy, and language which characterize real learning.

4. Integrate language skills and curriculum. Write for a copy of *Integrating Language Skills Into the Curriculum*, a 14-page model by Linda Azure and Beverly Wolf, at the Hamlin Robinson School, 10211 12th Avenue South, Seattle, WA 98168.

5. On index cards, write out brief descriptions of various situations or dilemmas: perhaps someone you don't like has invited you to come over; or you dropped the casserole on the floor, now the food is mixed with broken glass, and your guests are hungry for dinner; or a new kid has moved to town, and you would like to try to make friends. Put the cards in a paper bag. Let kids take turns picking one and telling what they would do.

6. Give plenty of chances for kids to act out the stories they hear. No training, no costumes; just let them hear the story once, and then as you reread it, let them act out all the parts or take the part of their favorite character. Plenty of roles to go around; no wrong answers.

acting out

7. Read a story without showing any pictures; ask kids to illustrate their favorite part.

drawing

8. Ask kids to list ten common rituals at home and at school, and pick likely vocabulary to accompany each one.

"*What not to do*"

9. Ask kids to list ten common taboos at home and at school, and pick likely vocabulary to accompany them.

10. Ask kids to write out ten phrases they each use frequently. What does the collection reveal about explanatory style?

Six Saboteurs
Language and Current Culture

If humans are naturally wired for language, why doesn't it always develop smoothly? In addition to the children with Specific Language Disability (see Chapter 3), all children today are affected by six cultural factors which sabotage language development. Does this mean that all children have language problems? No. But, because language is a medium of exchange among students—and between students and their teachers—whatever influences the language of some kids will have an effect on the language offered to and exchanged by the whole group. We can't say, "It's a bad leak. I'm glad it's not in my half of the boat."

This section is not meant to induce guilt trips. Who needs that kind of frequent-flyer mileage? However, we need to recognize the powerful effects of these factors in order to compensate for them.

The six factors are:

- weary parents
- day care
- caregivers
- ear infections and allergies
- the Golden Arches of McLanguage
- visual stimulation and instant gratification.

Weary Parents

Many well-intentioned, loving parents either don't understand their vital role in their offsprings' language development, or may be too tired at the end of the day to focus on words.

In 80% of two-parent families, both parents work. In single-parent families, the single parent almost always works. The parent who has worked all day—whether flipping burgers or arranging leveraged buyouts—is tired. The tired parent isn't likely to cross the threshold calling, "Come, my darling, let me read you a Hans Christian Andersen fairy tale." The grown-up is usually feeling "all talked out" and probably "all listened out," too. So, the affectionate parent gives a big hug and a tousle of the hair; says, "How goes it, kid?" or "Boy, am I glad to see you;" offers something to eat; flips through the mail and phone messages; and then turns on the TV to catch the news—or takes a shower and puts on comfortable clothes.

Let's not vilify working parents and deify those who stay home. They, too, grow weary: weary of small children's incessant demands and needs; the sound of little, high voices; or the obligations of the home office. Stay-home parents, like their office-bound counterparts, need to understand and nurture language development.

We know that language grows through intimacy, exchange, love, laughter, and exposure. We have seen how babies actively try to engage the adults they love in communication. And, while powerful communication can take place through Body English, children who don't receive linguistic stimulation from their parents miss out. Diminished exposure stunts growth. Even weary parents can find a little daily time or can focus on this over the weekend.

Day Care

Day care has made the job/no job difference for many families, and most day care workers and administrators are kind, well-meaning, and committed to the welfare of their charges. But, realistically, day care must provide physical safety in a tolerable level of noise. The adult/child ratio, the salary level for workers, the turnover in personnel, and the limited space in most facilities means that there is seldom time or space for the intimate fooling around with words—the cozy adult/child exchange—which cultivates both receptive and expressive language. Reality dictates otherwise.

Children who spend those early years, which are critical for language development, in day care are usually collected at the end of the day by weary parents. As we will see soon, these small children are also highly susceptible to colds or other contagions which affect their hearing. Thus, their language enrichment is thrice jeopardized.

Caregivers

Some working parents want their children to be cared for at home and hire sitters, nannies, au pairs, or whatever word is current in local terminology. Generally speaking, the pool of available workers is not highly educated and may speak English poorly (with accents or inaccuracies) or not at all. Loving, responsible, generous, and intuitive though these people may be, they cannot offer language models or enrichment.

Children's prime ages for language acquisition are between birth and five years. If their exposure is minimal, incorrect, or unintelligible during that time, their receptive language may develop poorly, and their expressive language will not find feedback.

Everett and Susan live in a medium-size city in the mid-West. Susan is a nurse-midwife at a nearby clinic, and Everett works for an electronics distributorship. They have an eighteen-month-old son named Eric, who is cared for at home by a woman of middle-European origin named Marta.

Part of the nearby mall is paved in cobblestones, and Eric loves to half-sing, half-exult when he is pushed over the cobblestones in his stroller. He loves what the motion does to his voice. And, he loves his stroller, which, in family argot, is called "the Strollie Rollie." He tries to say "strollie rollie" but can't quite get his tongue around it. Marta, with great exuberance, says, "Boy! Boy! Now! *Stonely Only!*"

Strollie Rollie makes linguistic sense; *stonely only* is gibberish. One label or mislabel doesn't matter; a daily diet does. Eric is learning what things are called, how to say words so others will understand him, how to join words together in grammatically correct sequence for English, how to sing and chant and say rhymes, and he is ready to play endless word games. He is at an age to soak up subject-verb agreement and morphology, which we considered in some detail on page 21. Given a loving but linguistically lousy model, his language growth will be slower than it otherwise would, slower than he deserves, and slow enough to have an effect on the two other circles: intellectual development and social/emotional development. The negative fallout may not show in school until he reaches third grade, but at that time he may begin to have trouble with inference, subtle aspects of comprehension, or handling volume.

Of course, children have been raised over the years by many loving people whose English is imprecise or whose language is not English. But, in days of yore, children were ringed around by siblings, parents were more accessible, grandparents often lived with them, schools taught vocabulary and grammar systematically, and good models abounded. Imprecision was counteracted.

Eric, so far, is an only child. He has breakfast with his parents, spends the whole day with Marta, and is bathed, read to, and put to bed by his parents. The ratio is about 5:1. Is Eric condemned to have words fail him? By no means. But, his parents need to understand what compensations are necessary. They need to get English lessons for Marta. They need to enroll her and Eric in the story hour at the nearby library. They need to get some cassettes of nursery rhymes and songs for the child to hear along with Marta. They need to make a conscious effort to include lots of language in the times they spend together on weekends.

Of course, parents are the most important caregivers, and some parents' mother tongue is not standard English. Dual language may be a blessing or a curse. For those who can acquire and expand their language skills easily, fluency in two or more languages may be no problem. However, we find innate language vulnerabilities in roughly 30% of the population, with males generally being more at risk than females. These children need to establish their mother tongue at least as far as the level of morphology, before being asked to understand and speak an additional language. If they are not fully developed in their native language, they will crest at the same level in the new language they are trying to learn. These rudimentary language levels will serve them adequately through early childhood, Sandcastles 105, and beginning reading and writing. But, these same language skills will not support the nuances of comprehension, the mysteries of poetry, the thrill of anticipation, or the exhilaration of discourse. Children thus hampered turn out not *bi-lingual* but *semi-lingual.*

Ear Infections and Allergies

As children go to nursery school at younger and younger ages, or as they attend day care, they are increasingly exposed to the bugs which cause colds, coughs, and other respiratory diseases. Though these are usually mild at the outset, in some children they progress to middle-ear infections, medically called OME (otitis media with effluent). In small children, the eustachian tube—which connects the ear with the inside of the nose and the throat—is narrow and also horizontal. As the child develops, the tube will increase in diameter and begin to slant downwards, effectively draining whatever fluid may have collected in the ear.

When a small child gets an ear infection, the first symptoms are pain and fever. The pediatrician looks and says, "Nasty ear there. Take this medicine until it's all gone, which will be ten days." The doctor often neglects to say, "Watch your child's hearing after all the symptoms are gone. Sometimes, fluid collects in the ear and causes depressed hearing on one or both sides. Your child will look rosy-cheeked and will sleep soundly, but inside a vital system is being impaired. Be on the alert."

Without symptoms, this condition is often unrecognized— sometimes for many years. What happens to a kid in high school with an unrecognized hearing loss in his right ear? His left ear may work fine, but suppose his desk puts his left ear to the window? What happens if he has 50% hearing and is seated at the back of the room? What happens if the teacher faces the board while talking, so the kids don't see her mouth? Kids who don't hear crisply have trouble paying attention, not to mention learning from lectures. Working backward, we can imagine what happens to kids in middle school with this unrecognized deficit. We can imagine only too well what befalls the afflicted but undetected lower school, kindergarten, or nursery school child.

Kids with recurrent ear infections and allergies need evaluation and help. The sooner, the better. Dr. Lynn Spivak,

Director of the Long Island Jewish Medical Center, says, "Even mild hearing loss can affect the development of a child's normal speech, language, and learning."

Allergies frequently exert a similar dampening or deadening effect on hearing, thus on language acquisition and exercise. For reasons no one seems to understand, the incidence of allergies in young children is on the gallop. Allergies cause "irritable tissue"—the suffering child may wiggle, squirm, and fidget as well as sneeze, blow, and say, "What?" The medicated child may fall asleep.

Helena—blonde, intelligent, and affectionate—had what seemed an unending series of ear infections from age one until the middle of second grade. Her delicate features were often underlined by dark shadows from congestion, wheezing, and resultant poor sleeping. Her reading was inaccurate and her spelling indecipherable. One day in third grade, she wrote for me, *I ngna tak rin letsis.* Although I have become an ace cryptographer over years of teaching, this one had me stumped. She explained, "I am going to (*I ngna*) take (*tak*) riding (*rin*) lessons (*letsis*)."

As ye hear, so shall ye speak; as ye speak, so shall ye write.

The Golden Arches of McLanguage

Humans are always looking for shortcuts. Linguistic shortcuts include gesture (holding out a plate of cookies), inflection ("more?"), telescoping (" 'later" for "see you later"), in-group shorthand ("you Granola-head").

I did some field work last Saturday at McDonald's. Inside, I saw a group of eighth graders milling around in eighth grade style: they were like an amoeba, with a definable nucleus but amorphous edges. Along came another "amoeba" of other eighth graders, who decided to go in and join group one. Here is their exchange in its entirety:

"Hi. 'S up?"
"Me neither."
"Big Mac?"
"Awesome."
"Uh huh."
"Fries?"
"Sure."
"Coke?"
"Good burps."
"Here?"
"'K."
"Hanuf?"
"Yeah."
"'S go."
"S' long."
"See ya."
"Bye"

Not one sentence was exchanged, but everyone understood "what's happ'nin', man."

These efficiencies are fine in small doses, but problems arise when verbal fast-foods make up the bulk of the child's linguistic diet. Kids need to hear and use the kind of language we want them to be able to read.

Visual Stimulation and Instant Gratification

In today's world, the media bombards us with pictures, and many children don't generate their own imagery.

In addition, we are all accustomed to satisfying our whims. Want music? Flip the switch. Want comedy, violence, or sitcom? Turn on the TV. Want ice water? Hit the gadget on the refrigerator door. Want heat? Nudge the thermostat. Want soup? Nuke it. Want information? Cruise Internet. Want contact? Phone home.

Kids ride a "Pushmepullyou" between cultural habit and academic requirement.

Want knowledge? Work for it. Want wisdom? Use words. Want skills? Choose present drudgery for future gain. Want the edge? Dig for information.

Language, by its very nature, delays gratification. Putting ideas or wants into words takes time, as does translating the words one hears into action. Granted, the time involved is a New York nano-second, but that's too long for lots of today's kids.

It goes without saying that the effects of poverty aggravate all the negatives of these factors, and make it harder for parents and children to compensate.

Kids who are negatively affected by the preceding six factors have what I call "apparent language." A delusion to both sender and receiver, it seems all right on the surface but lacks substance. Effective language is crisp and clear. It sits where it belongs, invites listeners to appropriate destinations, conveys that which is sought, and delivers what's needed. Soaring or solid, it is reliable.

So what are we supposed to do about all this?

1. The first step is heightened awareness. Many adults haven't catalogued these saboteurs and, thus, don't anticipate their influence on children's language development.

2. Compensate through additional language exposure and delight. All children will benefit; linguistically maimed children will heal. Through reading aloud, listening to tapes, reading alone, discussing and modeling, adults need to give kids rich experience with as many genres as possible. One teacher, saying the alphabet has 26 letters and the school year has 26 weeks, organized her language curriculum around autobiography, biography, columns, drama, etc.

3. Educators need to reach to and beyond the parents involved. We in schools should offer short training courses for caregivers. There will be five benefits:

o⟶ We will heighten awareness among the group who are children's constant companions.

o⟶ We will help caregivers dignify their own work by offering them professional training in a companionable setting. The course of four or five sessions (with presentation and discussion as part of each meeting) can conclude with a graduation ceremony, a certificate, and a simple celebration.

↦ Many caregivers had unpleasant experiences in school, themselves. They fear or mistrust the academic establishment. Bringing them in as partners dilutes negative feelings and gets these important people on our side.

↦ By exploring such topics as child development, language development, discipline, consistency, and communication, we reinforce consistency between home and school. This helps children feel safe and supported.

↦ By teaching this group where to find good local resources for language exposure (story hours at the library, tape clubs, craft and drama groups, play group projects, books on things to do with children), we help the caregivers improve their own language. Education owes this gift to our shadow partners.

4. Look at children's cumulative health histories. Those with patterns of recurrent ear infections need close scrutiny. How many, of what duration, what frequency, what after-effects?

5. Those with allergies need similar monitoring. Pay particular attention to asthma—a debilitating as well as frequently frightening condition which can drain children's energies away from the task at hand. An exhausted child will not reach out for language and play word games with the same zest as a rested one.

6. Listen to kids' spontaneous speech. Are they including verb tenses, spatial markers, degree endings, plural endings? If not, they need help.

7. Insure that kids are receiving instruction in both the structure and texture of language. Whole Language by itself won't provide the nuts and bolts; phonics alone will not provide the resonance of literature. For more information, see *Common Ground: Whole Language and Phonics Working Together* in the Resource Section.

8. Help people of all ages (65 isn't too late) acquire the language of strong emotions, so they can explain their feelings. Some people find this scary and need help and practice.

9. Keep the oral tradition alive. Story—heard and spoken—enriches language as it broadens understanding of human nature. NAPPS—National Association for the Preservation and Perpetuation of Storytelling (Jonesboro, TN)—offers books, tapes, instructions, conferences, and storytelling festivals. Children can both absorb and practice this ancient art.

10. Speak in complete sentences. Extend declarative sentences with dependent or parenthetical clauses. Encourage kids to speak in well-developed language. Listen and congratulate them when they do. Translate and model for them when they err.

Seven Rungs
The Language Ladder

L anguage growth is like a ladder. Children start at the bottom rung and—with luck—make it to the top.

Ladders are made of uprights called "rails," feet which hold the ladder in place where it touches the ground, and rungs which serve two functions. They bear the weight of the ascending climber, and they hold the rails parallel. With missing rungs—or ones too weak to bear weight—the rails would splay out, and the structure would sag or collapse.

The rungs of the language ladder work the same way.

Analogy
Categorization
Comparison
Description
Vocabulary
Exposure to words
Sensory apparatus & experience

Let's start with a top-down look, and then see what people need in order to climb back up.

○━ The top rung is analogy. Political science, comparative literature, mathematics, religion, history of art (to name but a few)—like all other higher-level intellectual endeavors—rest on the ability to think in analogy. Connections are the bedrock of thinking, and analogy is its highest form. This means moving beyond simply answering an analogy puzzle (such as hot:cold :: wet:?) and refers, rather, to the ability to use analogy to reason. An article in Scientific American from October, 1994 quotes Stanislaw Ulam's Meditation on Creative Thought: "...And what we call talent or perhaps genius itself depends to a large extent on the ability to use one's memory properly to find the analogies...[which] are essential to the development of new ideas."

transference

○━ In order to think in analogy, one must be able to categorize. Through categorization, we establish the mental file folders from which to draw our analogies.

○━ In order to categorize, we need to be able to compare. Comparison allows us to sort, which is prerequisite to filling the mental file folders of categorization.

○━ In order to compare, we must be able to describe.

○━ To describe, we need vocabulary.

○━ To acquire vocabulary, we must have exposure to words, ideally in an emotionally benevolent climate.

○━ To absorb words and what they represent, we must have intact sensory apparatus and experience.

Now, bracing the rails of our ladder against the walls of linguistic challenge—and adjusting the feet for stability—let's see what the rungs themselves are made of and how they do their job. We will remember that developing children, rocket scientists, and octogenarians scramble all over these rungs all the time. We are not talking about one-stop shopping.

Sensory Apparatus and Experience

Growing children, experiencing the world through their five senses, establish memories and concepts. They *see* people, objects, backgrounds, movement, edges, and colors, and begin to understand perspective. They *hear* near and distant sounds, differentiate between loud and soft or harsh and pleasing ones, and separate environmental noises from conversational rumbles and ripples. They *smell* food, perfume, their mother's skin, their father's after-shave lotion, the dog's coat, and the smells which distinguish each dwelling place from every other one. They *touch* their mother's cheek, their father's stubble, the plush of stuffed animals, the squish of porridge, the refreshment of water. They *taste* whatever they can get their hands on. Learning much of their environment through their mouths, they gum plastic toys, suck on bottles and pacifiers, and teach their tongues through the warmth and sweetness of milk, the cool of juice, the bitterness of vitamin drops, the almost-sourness of pureed fruits, or the sogginess of cookies.

As mentioned in the previous chapter, hearing impairments are easy to overlook. No neon light blinks on the child's forehead, no bone protrudes through the skin; rashes and blisters don't cover the body. Yet, there is no way to overestimate the role of hearing in language development; diminished hearing does the work of termites on the first rung. Of all the senses mentioned, hearing is the most integral to normal language development. Teachers need to teach parents about the linguistic aspects of hearing disorders, and reawaken themselves to higher levels of vigilance concerning the students in their care.

Exposure to Words, and Emotional Climate

Humans absorb words—connecting vocabulary, experience, and emotion. If the emotional climate is warm and nurturing, the child with intact language capacity will bring sensory events, the abstractions of words, and the coziness of contentment into a central matrix from which language will grow.

Solemnity isn't necessary. Young children delight in silliness, alliteration, rhymes, repetitive refrains, nonsense words. Language is there for them to bend, change, tip over, turn inside-out, invent, take apart, put together, and own. Early delight in wordplay augurs later delight in reading. Early avoidance of language prefigures distaste for reading, difficulty with writing, and probable deficits in communication. Obviously, then, we need to notice those children who are not interested in the stories we tell, the conversation we offer, or the books we read aloud.

Some children need to have their motor systems in gear before language can seep in. Forced to sit with hands folded, maintaining eye contact, they are overwhelmed or bored. Allowed to play with their toy trucks or bits of Lego—vroom, vroom, vroom—they can pay attention to language using other parts of their brains. I heard this exchange in a classroom last week:

"Tommy, please pay attention to the story."

"Vroom! Vroom! I am."

"You can't be. You're too busy with your car. You need to know what the dragon did."

"I heard. He ate the worser monster."

Conversely, some children fool us into equating steady eye contact with comprehension. In my first teaching assignment, I was asked to explain the mysteries of multiplication to a confused third grader. Using no manipulatives, no pictures, and nothing which the child could see, touch, or move, I proceeded in my beginner's ignorance to talk her through the purpose of multiplying. She gazed at me unswervingly as I droned on and on. Finally, I was finished.

She said, "May I ask you a question?"

"Certainly, my child," I oozed.

Still looking right at me, she asked, "Do you always have chapped lips?"

Vocabulary

Children connect words with good, bad, tasty, lonely, splashy, hungry, thirsty, and satisfied moments. They also connect words with people. Once this is done, they have the gridwork on which to slot all manner of new vocabulary and expressions—first receptively, then expressively. The sense of power which comes from knowing what to call things spurs them on to learn new terms. Children can remember the past, experience the present, and anticipate the future when they possess the vocabulary of their lives.

School-age children do not learn vocabulary by studying lists, looking up definitions, and writing sentences. They do learn those new words which "hover at the rim of experience."[1] As we lead students into new realms and concepts, we can help them grasp the vocabulary which matches their explorations and new powers.

Description

Accurate description uses the 6 *wh* comprehension words: *who, what, when, where, why,* and *how.* It also uses markers of time and space: *early this morning, a year ago, next week, over there, under the sofa, along the side of the road.* The language of physical properties is an integral part of description: the *large, prickly* fruit; the *smelly* sneaker; the *slippery, satin* dress; or the *rough sawn* cedar siding. Additionally, it embraces emotional connotations: my *best* friend, a *screaming* cat fight, a *joyful* frolic, a *dismal* happenstance.

Timid children will stick to such limpid descriptions as *nice, pretty, good,* and *bad.* Braver souls—who in Star Trek terminology "dare to boldly go..."—move into juicier adjectives and more powerful adverbs: *delicate, fragile, fragrant, obedient, flexible, wicked, outrageous, evil, rancid, sour,* or *rapidly, excitedly, enthusiastically, grumpily, rudely, gleefully.* Where do linguistically adventurous thinkers, speakers, and writers get their vivid, punchy descriptors? Readers of this book know the answer:

- from exposure

- through benevolent contagion

- by example.

Reading Specialist Dolores Durkin is famous for saying, "Language is more caught than taught."

Comparison

Incorporating description, comparison moves one rung higher on the ladder. It depends partly on morphology (the pronouns, plurals, and singulars—those seemingly inconsequential little endings of degree, space, and time we met earlier in Chapter 2). In addition, comparison draws from orderly filing. People who can compare the different reactions of people being kept waiting in a restaurant, or the contents of the last five exams given by Mrs. Newman, or twelve objects—all of which are fuzzy and none of which are the same—pluck their verbal equipment from associative networks deep in the brain. People who store their experiences sensibly can retrieve them efficiently and use them comparatively.

To ornament experience with the vocabulary of comparison is the joy of poets: "It is a beauteous evening, calm and free, the holy time is quiet as a Nun breathless with adoration."[2] Simile floats ideas: "I wandered lonely as a cloud, that floats on high o'er vales and hills."[3] Metaphor taps the creator's imagination as it offers imagery to the receiver: "a necklace of suburbs" or "On Chromoluminism. Where does a European go when he is 'lost in thought'? Seurat...the old dazzler...has painted that place. It lies on the other side of attention, a long, lazy boat ride from here."[4]

Categorization

Categorizing really means recognizing combinations, collecting patterns, sorting similarities and differences, and stepping up to "multiple entry" thinking. It is no accident that the verbal sub-test most predictive of conceptual ability on the I.Q. test known as the WISC lll is called "Similarities." In this, the subject is asked to say how two objects are the same and how they are different. An example might be *canal* and *river*. Determining that both fit the *body of water* category, the listener must know the meanings of the words *canal* and *river*. To say how they differ, the speaker must have both the concept and word *manmade*, and some other descriptive vocabulary such as *wide, narrow, deep, shallow, current, swirling, eddy, tidal, calm,* or *brackish.* Vocabulary feeds thought; thought elicits vocabulary.

Neurologists, philosophers, and others who study human consciousness are delineating what they call "convergence zones,"[5] areas of thought in which we collect experiences, ideas, and knowledge, bringing them to bear on concepts or puzzles at hand. The greater one's supply of language, the more varied the possible offerings, and the richer the mix will be when they come together in a convergence zone. Categorization and the skills preceding it lead to convergence zones, just as convergence zones open the door to analogy.

Analogy

Analogy explores relationships. Ideas may be related by opposites (hot : cold), by meaning as in synonym and antonym (tasty : delicious, tasty : revolting), by spelling pattern (puddle

96

: middle), by time or space (serf : middle ages or Massachusetts : Rhode Island), by property (tiny : ant), by metaphor (Leonard Bernstein : the Northern Lights), by association (Houdini : illusion), by subject matter (addition : subtraction), by profession (George Eliot : writer), by rhyme (mad : sad), by alliteration (three throbbing thrushes : seven sulking sisters), or by any other connective device. Step one is to see the relationship in the introductory pair.

Shouldn't this come before categorizatn & maybe even comparison?

Step two is to continue the pattern:

- tasty : delicious:: sweet smelling : fragrant

- tasty : revolting:: soft : hard

- puddle : middle :: wriggle : haggle

- serf : middle ages :: astronaut : space age

- Massachusetts: Vermont :: California : Oregon

- tiny : ant :: huge : elephant

- Leonard Bernstein : Northern Lights :: Vivaldi : rainbow

- Houdini: illusion :: Thomas Edison : clarity

- addition : subtraction :: multiplication : division

- George Eliot : writer :: Frank Lloyd Wright : architect

- mad : sad :: face : lace

- three throbbing thrushes : seven sulking sisters :: huge hollow hunks : very vague values.

Or, try:

love : marriage :: happiness : ?

Step three is to use such conceptual patterns and see their logical extensions. While this is high intellectual function, it need not be limited to adult scholars. A fifth grader, who had been studying mythology and folk tales, wrote, "The death of Baldar made bad things happen. The opening of Pandora's box released evil. Some of the bad things they had in common were: lies, drudgery, and old age."

Thinking in analogy, the height of verbal abstraction, is the top rung of the ladder and the summit of thought. If this is so, and if we want as many students as possible to be comfortable at this level, we need to look with care and caution at the condition of the rungs preceding it on the language ladder. We must bend our best efforts to see that the lower rungs are strong, that they hold the rails together, and that they are resilient to the steps of questing humans.

So what are we supposed to do about all this?

1. Create a positive emotional climate.

2. Provide wide, deep, joyful exposure to words.

3. Play with word patterns.

4. Use variety in our own vocabularies.

5. Describe precisely.

6. File systematically.

7. Compare judiciously.

8. Categorize broadly.

9. Converge originally.

10. Think analogously.

Eight Functions
"It's Only Human"

"It's only human" to enjoy the fruits of language; as far as we know, we're the only species that can create and use this powerful and beautiful abstraction on so many sophisticated and diverse levels. Let's examine eight functions:

- filing and retrieving
- establishing a boundary
- exchanging information
- exercising a remarkable capacity
- exploring cause and effect
- linking emotion and behavior
- experiencing the power of story
- developing Executive Function.

Filing and Retrieving

Language is our sorter. When our experiences and perceptions are jumbled together, we have a hard time retrieving what we need. It may be in papers on the desk, the contents of a school backpack, or household effects.

In defense of meta-language

Once, years ago, when our four children produced dirty laundry with the same dependability they ate the last cookies in the cupboard, I fell ill with the flu. My husband kindly offered to "manage everything." He took underwear, dishtowels, new blue jeans, white blouses, red towels, oily rags, black socks, soccer uniforms, tie dies, batiks, and a bedspread and put them in the washer.

One child came wailing down the stairs, "Dad! Where's my soccer stuff? I need it for today's game."

"I washed it. Don't worry, I'll get it out right now. There's plenty of time to dry it." Within a minute of opening the washer, he looked like Laäcoon. Pulling the twisted items from the machine, draping them around his neck as he searched, he appeared as if he were being strangled by serpents. Untwisting a towel, he would locate one sock. Where was the mate? Inside the bedspread—now a color no manufacturer ever dreamed of—were the red shorts. "Only a shirt and sock to go. They went in, so they've got to come out, right?" Anyone who's ever done the laundry knows the answer to that.

Through language, we can use time, space, properties, emotion, and people to sort and file: *the day before yesterday, on the top shelf, the shiny one, that scary time, everyone in our family.* If our language system is strong enough to support this unconscious activity, we can retrieve what we need for anecdotes, working memory, or planning: the day before yesterday the dry cleaning wasn't ready, so I'll pick it up today; I remember putting the picnic hamper on the top shelf; that black purse isn't the right size, I'd better take the shiny one; I remember how scared I got last time I came back into that dark, empty house, so this time I'll take the flashlight; everyone in our family loves strawberries, so I'll get a double batch.

Because we multiple-list-cross-file without even giving it a thought, we bring variety to our convergence zones. Variety allows those unexpected combinations we call "new ideas" or "creativity." Educators and parents need to budget time for this capacity to grow and develop.

Establishing a Boundary

One of the central jobs of early childhood is to establish the boundary between reality and fantasy. This doesn't necessarily mean we want less or more of either one, but we want the child to know—stomach-pit certain—which is which. Why? The small child believes "Everything is possible." The flip side of that coin is "Anything could happen." Children cannot distinguish the ludicrous from the probable until the reality/fantasy border is in place. Until they can distinguish the logical from the impossible, they can't order their universe. Until their universe is stable, they can't predict where safety and danger lie. Until they can make that prediction, they are at the mercy of upcoming events, rather than being in some control of their destiny. Because this boundary is invisible and intangible, language is the only tool to construct it.

Language helps do this job as the child asks, "Is this real or pretend?" "Could this really happen?" or "Has a real live person ever met a dragon?" Of course, we do not denigrate the power and importance of pretending; the child just needs to know what is real and what is make-believe. Most children establish this boundary by the end of kindergarten, and its appearance is one of the markers indicating that the child is ready to learn in a group.

I once taught a child I think of as Wolf Boy. He had grown up in financially privileged but emotionally sterile circumstances. Spending most of his time alone and silent in the woods, his lunch being brought to him on a tray by a non-English-speaking caregiver, he would play among the squirrels, ride his bike on the garden paths, build dirt roads, and make twig garages for his toy cars and trucks. His parents would occasionally chat with him when they dropped in—between work and the evening's activity—but more often supper would be served to him, again on a tray, in front of the TV. His bank account was as bloated as his language was shriveled. He came to school unpracticed, apprehensive, able to amuse himself for hours and therefore mistrustful of the regimens of the school day, and yearning for affection but afraid of human contact.

I taught him to read. One day, thinking I was offering him a great treat, I opened up a book of silly poems. There on the page was a picture of a decapitated man holding his smiling-faced head in his hands. Wolf Boy turned white with fear and, trembling, said, "Don't ever show me that again."

Exchanging Information

Through language, we can communicate what we have heard, read, thought, or felt. Via voice, print, paragraphs, graphs, or numbers, we open kingdoms of discourse, discus-

sion, persuasion, and explanation, as well as the murky excitement of ambiguity and the ability to hold conflicting ideas in
our heads—probing each as we compare and contrast.

Although many people think of exchanging information
primarily as a verbal opportunity, it is equally part of reading
and writing. The writer and the reader exchange information
and reactions.

In *Finding the Heart of the Child,* Edward Hallowell—physi-
cian, author, philosopher, poet, sage, and lover and guardian of
language—says it this way: "With other art forms, the beauty is
already out there, external; that is, the beauty resides outside
the mind, in the painting hanging on the wall, or on the film
projected on the screen, or in the sound made by the instru-
ments. But, leaving aside the tonal beauty of the words, the
beauty they create is entirely internal. We never speak of a
beautiful poem and mean that it looks beautiful on the page.
We mean that the images it induces us to create in our own
brains are beautiful. Words connect us to the dormant creator
within us all. In a true sense, as we read a novel we write it ourselves, we create it for ourselves, image by image, character by
character, melody by melody."[1]

Language is the tool for organizing the volume and variety of
what we take in. As we learned on the rungs of the language
ladder, we acquire vocabulary, we describe, compare, categorize, and think in analogy.

Many students, particularly those with potential or talent in
the three-dimensional spheres, have trouble organizing what
they hear, what they read, what they speak, and particularly what

they write. We have seen some of the reasons for this in earlier chapters, but this is a good place to reiterate that these kids profit from the methods and materials originally designed for the L.D. population, which are entirely suitable for all children.

These kids are often keenly alert to color, design, shape, and internal machinery. But, for them, large collections of words are a confusing mass; they don't know where, how, or—sometimes—why to sort the material. Simply telling a kid like this to "Be more organized, please," is like saying, "Have a better personality." If they knew how, they would have done it already.

In addition to organizing, some bright kids have trouble with rate of processing. They can bite, chew, swallow, and digest small snacks, but a full dinner makes them sick. These kids need to work in small segments; they often need time extensions; they need to see why what they've just done matters, and where to stash it.

Mel Levine coined the phrase "lethal cluster" to describe the collective effect of mild disorders. For example, a student might have a minor weakness in auditory memory (remember the short tape?), a mild small-motor problem which makes sustained handwriting awkward or painful, occasional inaccuracies in decoding multi-syllabic words—particularly under pressure of time or performance, and a soggy set of organizational skills. One at a time, they are not alarming; but put that child in a classroom where he is asked to listen, reason, remember, copy from the board, read complex directions, and produce a summary, and the lethal cluster will kill his spirit as well as butcher his academic performance.

With the kind of materials mentioned in the Resource Section, we can help these kids *use* language to *control* and *tame* language.

Exercising a Remarkable Capacity *Asking questions.*

Are humans the only creatures who can formulate a question? Children who exercise this native ability—and who are encouraged to continue this time-consuming, mind-nourishing activity in the sacred confines of the school day—are keeping open the doorways to discovery and gateways to knowledge.

Sometimes, particularly when class sizes are big, time seems short. The prospect of units-to-cover blankets chances-to-think. Educators register a definite preference for the tidiness of answers over the messiness of questions. But, in succumbing to this preference, we condemn our students to live in other people's discoveries.

One of my mentors grew up in Chicago. She was a tiny child who wore wire-rimmed glasses from her earliest years. Her homeward route from school took her through vacant lots where there was nothing to block the winter winds coming off the lake. The cold would make the wire of her glasses bite into her cheeks and across her temples. She would run as fast as she could. When he heard her coming, her father, an enormously tall Rabbi, would open the door, holding his arms out wide. She would jump into them, and as he enfolded her, he would say, "Leah, did you ask any good questions in school today?" // Quite a change from "What did you get on the science test?"

Exploring Cause and Effect

Passionate curiosity propels growing children to discover the secrets of cause and effect. Is there a little man under the mat who swings the supermarket door open as you approach? Is there a miniature Patrick Stewart inside the television set? Why does the moon get smaller and bigger? As children prowl around, unlocking the secrets of their universe, they are guided by what they see, hear, smell, taste, touch. This means their reason is limited by their five senses. Language allows them to study the forces and penetrate the mysteries which lie beyond sensory thresholds. Without the language of explanation, they are left thinking that things "just happen."

One young lady of five lived in a multi-generational family. Her grandparents spoke only Portuguese. Her parents spoke both Portuguese and English, and she spoke only English. She said, "When I get older of being grown up, I'll get Portuguese." She thought of it as being like gray hair and wrinkles, a property which grew along with *Anno Domini*.

Linking Emotion and Behavior

Humans use language for mediating, reasoning, and governing their actions and reactions.

➤ Language helps us mediate: shall I eat that Brownie now, or would I rather have ice cream after dinner?

➤ Language helps us reason our way through problems: if the United States has threatened military strikes as a consequence of violating the agreement, will reluctance to use force be seen as weakness or strength?

o—т Language gives us brakes on our behavior: telling children who are upset with life or angry with others to "Use your words" lets them know that their grievances will be aired and heard, that words can stall off bloodshed, and that solutions can be reached through the miracles of language. Think of classrooms, playgrounds, commuter parking lots, corporate board rooms, the Oval Office, or faculty meetings. Hunter/ warriors turn into bargainer/threatener/cajolers: "I'll be your best friend if..."

Pre-verbal or unpracticed children *see, want, take.* As the codes of civilization develop inside them, they *see, want, ask,* and sometimes *take* anyway. As the language of negotiation grows, they are able to *see, want, ask, bargain,* and *get* in the long run: if I let you have the red ball for a long turn, will you let me use your street-hockey stick? As the language of long-term planning joins that of short-term wishes, people can *see, want, ask, plan,* and *get*: the profit projections show that if we capitalize on this division and invest heavily in developing our other plant, we will find ourselves strong on both fronts at the end of our five-year plan.

Language is a tool for dealing with the impulsivity of Attention Deficit Disorder. But, kids need to learn the vocabulary. Many language-weak or linguistically underexposed children don't glom on to such words as *later, until, after, first, then, finally.* These, obviously, are the language of the postponement of gratification, the *sine qua non* of school learning. Teaching them to ADD children through modeling, frequent use, games, and role playing can help these kids develop the brakes that allow mutual enjoyment between them and their worlds.

Experiencing the Power of Story

The word *enchant* comes from French and means, literally, to wrap in song. Story and language, singing together, give purpose to enjoyment—and enjoyment to purpose.

Through language, therefore through story, we are led to throb with sympathy, laugh with scorn, shiver with terror, gloat with superiority, glow with romance, admire with fervor, or love with abandon, all without leaving our seats.

We travel the territories of fiction, we construct and reconstruct our own histories, we prefigure our tomorrows, and we tell other people what we think of them by the words, intonations, and constructions we use when we talk to them. Children use the stories we concoct to help them learn who they are. We know from common sense and daily living that story has the power to soothe, mold, inspire, and force. Such power needs reverence and gentle, wise handling.

Several years ago, a third grade boy came to our school in the middle of the year. Danish-speaking, bright, and eager, he made friends easily but struggled over reading and writing, not to mention speaking and listening. Trying to get some of the particulars of his language profile, I asked him if he knew the story of the Three Bears. "Ya," he assured me. So, I asked him to tell it to me. Through his error, he unwittingly gave me a powerful metaphor of what schooling ought to be.

He told me about the animals, the forest, and the little girl with yellow hair, although he couldn't remember her name. He got her into the Bears' house, had her go first to the chairs, and told what happened. Next, he told about the bedroom, and he knew what happened there, too. Finally, he took her into the kitchen. "There," he said proudly, "she saw three bowls of *courage*. The first bowl of courage was too hot, and it burned her mouth. The second bowl was too cold and tasted bad. But, the third bowl was just right, and so she ate it all up."

Language can prepare that nourishing, satisfying bowl of courage.

Developing Executive Function

Executive function, the CEO of the language brain, describes the human ability to formulate an idea, make a plan, anticipate the steps needed to carry out the plan, predict which materials will be necessary, know where and how to collect them, allot time for the plan (or segments of it), begin, monitor progress, know what's been accomplished and what remains to be done, hang with it, be able to interrupt and return as reality dictates, and recognize the finish line. As a way of structuring and remembering this, pediatric neurologist Martha Denckla uses the name of the Egyptian deity ISIS:

I = **Initiate.** Can the person marshall the material and the intellectual, psychological, and physical forces to get going?

S = **Sustain.** Can the person sustain interest, concentration, focus? Obviously, this is where some people with ADD, wanting desperately to sustain their focus, get in trouble.

I = **Inhibit.** Can the person inhibit visual, auditory, somatic, motor, or psychological distractions? The sight of another student walking around in the classroom, the sound of a group going by in the hall, hungry stomach rumblings, allergic itchy noses, or daydreaming—the silent thief of concentration—may derail someone who is trying very hard.

S = Shift. Can the person shift away from the task at hand, pack it up in mental file folders, do something else for a while, and then return? Students in school are asked to do this all day long, as classes come in 40- or 45-minute modules. They are expected to arrive, immerse themselves in the topic, reason, remember, and often write, summarize, stop, change classrooms, and do the same thing all over again. They are asked to shift sets, change lexicons, and break and re-focus attention with the speed and accuracy of Irish sword dancers. While many of the strategies to help the ADD population emphasize focus, very few teach the transitional strategies required to shift.

How do we use Executive Function? Students plan homework, long-term assignments, or pizza parties. Parents plan the choreography of work, home maintenance, family time, and recreation. Lawyers plan strategies, schedule appointments, and usually run over the time they've saved for writing a brief. Educators plan the layout of the school year, long-term curriculum chunks, short-term emphasis, immediate activities, parent conferences, class projects, time for discussions, and chances to have fun. To do any of these requires an accurate understanding of time.

Many young people in today's digital era can call out numbers ("It's 10:22."), which creates the impression that they know how to tell time—and understand what the numbers mean. Unfortunately, many do not understand that time is both *linear* and *circular*, and don't know how to use this powerful organizer.

Time is *linear* when we look at a time line, and when we sort our lives into present, past, and future. I purposely used that sequence, because it matches the way the concept of time develops in the learning child. To sense the present isn't much of a trick. The child then learns to distinguish between the present and the past—both the recent and the distant past. Thus:

distant past   recent past   X (the person now)

Once that mechanism is in place, the child has the equipment to anticipate the future. Thus, the kingdom of planning opens, joining the kingdom of memory as possible alternative destinations when moving in either direction from the immediate present. Thus:

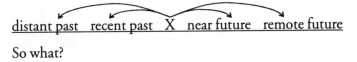

distant past   recent past X near future remote future

So what?

Children cannot postpone gratification unless and until they can make logical anticipations of the future. A kid who doesn't understand *in ten minutes* would be a fool to put aside something of immediate interest. Someone unable to grasp *hard work now for great gain later* will not be able to study in the library instead of going to the movies.

Time is *circular* in its repetitive cycles: seconds, minutes, hours, days, weeks, seasons, years. To my horror, I find that a large number of students—apple-cheeked and some with hefty trust funds—in third grade and on up don't know the days of the week in order, and can say nine or ten months, but not the whole twelve in sequence.

In one glitzy California school, the eighth grade teacher said, "Well, that might be true of your kids back East, but not our kids. You see, they're affluent..." (rhyming with en-glue'-ment). I asked his permission to chat with some of his students during their free time. Of four eighth graders, three could say the days of the week, but one said them as though they were all one word: "Munny-Toozdee-Wenzee-Thurzee-Friey-Sardee-Sunee." The suffix "day" never made the list. Without using fingers or the calendar, one of the four could not tell me what day comes between Tuesday and Thursday, two of the four could not tell me what day comes three days after Tuesday, and none of the four could say without thinking hard what day comes four days before Friday.

So what?

If you don't know what day comes three days after Tuesday, and your assignment is due in three days, you don't know whether you have to hand it in before the weekend or after. Executive Function depends on using the concept of time.

One of the most valuable and least discussed aspects of time is something called *elapsing time*. Having a sense of elapsing time helps you get things finished: if I have 20 minutes to do this, I'd better hurry. Asked to write about the causes of the

Civil War for an hour, a student without an accurate sense of elapsing time doesn't know how fast to go, how much to include or omit, and when it's time to stop writing new words and look over what's already produced.

Key aspects of time are invisible, accessible *only* through language. Children with innately weak language systems—or who are under-exposed and under-taught—may be missing this vital organizing tool, but their facility in calling out the numbers on digital watches camouflages their serious linguistic lapse.

Furthermore, as we saw in Chapter 3, many people who are powerful in the three-dimensional realms—generally associated with right hemisphere of the brain—are wired with "a climate inhospitable to language." The right hemisphere of the brain has no mechanism at all for the comprehension, monitoring, or memory of time. People whose preferred mode of thinking draws heavily on right-hemisphere function usually need visual aids and extra instruction to harness the tool of time. We know from the lore of famous people's mistakes that many brilliant thinkers are habitually tardy, forget which evening they have a dinner date, and miss wedding anniversaries.

So what are we supposed to do about all this?

1. We owe it to all kids from third grade on up to probe their understanding of time: telling time, marking time, using time, and sensing and recording elapsing time. Chapter 10 describes a book students can assemble about themselves with their own information about time.

2. Educators and parents need to train themselves to use visual aids and manipulative materials when explaining concepts or giving directions. This will help all children—particularly those with processing problems, those with attentional issues, and those whose curiosity is strong but whose language is weak.

3. Adults should be sure to budget generous slices of time for kids to ask questions, as well as to listen to answers. We need, then, to save time to ponder and answer their questions, and to provide time for the next round. Time. Time. Time. It comes up all the time.

4. Use language to strip away the mysteries of cause and effect.

5. Teach children the underpinnings of Executive Function, and help them identify which they are using, when, and why, as well as how these activities help.

6. Be alert to four language-dependent abilities which ready children bring to formal academics. Educators see increasing numbers of students who are chronologically ready to hang out with their peers, but unready for abstract, language-based group learning. Unready children, like disabled children, influence the academic level of the classroom. Sad to say, well up into junior high and high school, we are dealing with kids who have not solidified these four abilities:

- the ability to sit still and concentrate
- the ability to learn and use a symbol system
- the ability to postpone gratification
- the ability to distinguish between reality and fantasy.

The ability to sit still and concentrate requires a strong sense of elapsing time, psychological availability for schoolwork, the ability to focus, and the ability to shift.

7. Encourage the ability to learn and use a symbol system. This requires appropriate instruction, knowledge of sound/symbol correspondence, recognition of sight words, AND the internal language to make the process worth the trouble.

8. Reinforce the ability to postpone gratification, explored in this chapter and elsewhere. It depends on having the language skills, temporal organization, and willpower to understand and govern oneself with such words as *later, soon, in ten minutes,* or *not until.* The mind-set represented by the term is vital for delivering oneself to new tasks.

9. Cultivate the ability to distinguish between reality and fantasy. This is one of the important differences between the student who can sit in a group, learning alongside peers, and the child who cannot.

10. Play with language—humor is contagious; power is intoxicating.

Nine Danger Signs
Warnings, Wishes, and Washouts

When language serves us well, we are eloquent lovers, clear delegators, organized planners, articulate problem solvers, congenial conversationalists, inspiring teachers, humorous commentators, passionate advocates, persuasive orators, and readable writers. When we are careless with the passepartout—leaving it out in the rain to rust, misplacing it, bending its indentations by using it to pry off bottle caps, dulling its precision, or ignoring it and trying to jimmy doors and pick locks instead—we lose the power language could bestow. Since language disruptions don't come with blinking lights, how do we know when things are, glory, *awry*?

Here are nine danger signs:

1. "What?"

2. Word Distance

3. Strands Out Of Synch

4. Arrhythmias

5. Disorganization

6. Inappropriate Behaviors

7. Misunderstandings

8. Forgetfulness

9. Malapropisms, Spoonerisms, and Galimatias

We will consider possible remedies in the "So what are we supposed to do about all this?" section at the end of this chapter. Chapter 10 will also offer specific suggestions. So, help follows, but this section is designed to ring the alarm.

"What?"

Since children are curious by nature—and are constantly trying to figure out their world and what makes it operate—they soak up as much information as they can through their ears. Impaired hearing cuts off access. When people of any age frequently say, "What?" they are literally telling us they need to have their hearing checked.

Too many times, parents return from a visit to the doctor saying, "He says not to worry. He gave Jimmy this little office test and says things are mostly in the normal range. We should come back in a month, if we're still concerned." Reduced hearing during the years which are critical for language development (birth through five) leads to immediate language impoverishment, which overshadows future academic work and learning.

Word Distance

The child who is uninterested in hearing stories told or read aloud is either telling us that sounds and words aren't getting in, or that they're getting in but don't have meaning, or that too many are coming in all at once. When narrative—or simply looking at a picture book and learning and practicing what things are called—doesn't captivate the child, adults need to notice and find out more. Some kids are "word distant." Oblivious to the fun, they remove themselves to other activities.

Here are some comments teachers or parents may make:

- "Sam prefers actions to words."
- "Genevieve keeps to herself."
- "Joey often doesn't respond when I talk to him."
- "When I read a story to the class, I feel as if Fernando's on the moon."
- "He makes plenty of truck and animal noises; it's just words he doesn't use."

The balance of boys' and girls' names is intentional. Brain research shows that many aspects of language are more robust, flexible, and mutually supportive in the female, and that males are more susceptible to language disorders. My personal experience in over twenty-three years of full-time teaching bears this out. Of course, some girls have language problems, too, but the ratio pans out at about 4:1.

These kids, like those with reduced hearing, often say, "What?"

Word-distant people don't enjoy wordplay. This may result from underexposure to the idea or lack of opportunity. Think back, for instance, to the six saboteurs in Chapter 6. Although sound play begins as a solitary sport, wordplay requires participation.

What is wordplay, anyway? Rhyming, making up new words, alliteration, refrains, or "word trains"—in which the last sound in one word is the first sound in the next (*music/kaleidoscope/popsicle/lizard*)—are typical examples. Wordplay is open-ended; there are no rights and wrongs; energy and humor are the fuel; enjoyment is the goal.

Absence of wordplay can also stem from avoidance or aversion. Some kids avoid word games because they don't see the point and would rather be doing something they actively enjoy. A few have a genuine aversion. These are kids who just can't do it. Their language systems betray them if they try.

Enticement is what's needed—seduction by sounds, delight by success.

Strands Out of Synch

Normally, receptive and expressive language grow together, reinforcing the other. The progression may look like this:

⟶ From birth to one year, the child starts to recognize and localize sounds, responds to his or her name, understands "No," and obeys (or disobeys) simple commands. In output, the child babbles, mimics, and may intentionally say a word or two.

⊶ In the next six months, the child begins to identify some body parts, toys, and people. Most children in this age range have a vocabulary ranging from 3 to 50 words.

⊶ At age two, most children can carry out verbal commands, have vocabularies of 50 or more words, and can join two words together.

⊶ Children at two-and-one-half can follow two-step directions, and their vocabulary grows more rapidly at this stage than at any other time of life. Most can deliver three-, four-, or five-word sentences.

⊶ At three, most children understand the language around them, including verbs, nouns, pronouns, prepositions, and adjectives. Their vocabularies are around 1,000 words, and their output has the organization of adult language.

⊶ The four-year-old responds easily to speech, uses correct syntax, can manage past and future tenses, and can describe objects and relate events.

⊶ By five, most children have a fully formed language system. Of course, it will grow, but as an internal system it has all the components in their proper places. Except for some articulation tangles, five-year-olds' speech is intelligible, resting on solid grammatical foundations.

⊶ The six-year-old can repeat a twelve-syllable sentence, can produce almost all sounds correctly, uses five- or six-word sentences, and has a vocabulary of roughly 2,500 words.[1]

As mentioned in previous chapters, speaking and writing are windows on internal process. If children take in tangled language, that's what they'll give out. My friend, a first grade student with Specific Language Disability, says the best Christmas Carol of all is "No Way In A Manger."

If receptive language outstrips expressive capacity, the kid will understand everything, but give back halting, sparse, or "factory outlet" responses.

If expressive language outstrips receptive (which seldom happens), the child will have voluminous, repetitive output. The child may chant the same song or nursery rhyme over and over—the way we all do (silently) when we "get a tune on the brain" and can't escape.

In learning disabled children, we may see valiant effort, good information, and expressive intent culminate in writing which requires a Rosetta Stone to decipher. Here, unaltered, is a composition by a third grader who had been learning about the life of Mozart. I have translated it into accurate English below, but readers should try to untangle it on their own, seeing and hearing the sounds running in wild confusion in the child's head.

MY Vigin of Omadais Modart

A long long time ogo a geanuis was born and his familey named him Mosort. he cood play the peauano his sister Nanurl she was. A genius to won day papa said we our going to Englin Mosort and Nanurl they wor icstereaealis icsideid Modert and Nanurl never have bin on a bate. At Englin at the palis the can bocter said to odeins these chinds our a genius and woch and lisin well. Modort played they best and Nanurl did to. The odeais cord Modert a mericl boy. A cupel days after Mosart made his first sinfiney and the they went to Paris. And won day a nuther mugishin came. Masart fent so good that he is talking to a men thats alot betr then him. Nanurl was geting onder and Mosart was to. Masart made a Oprou some pepeol thenk it is papa is riting is mucic four him whun day A mushishin come to test in Mosart. After wers the mushishin tond the that town. saw ever the pepaol now no whon dosit think that Mosart's papa dosit rite his music. Mosart was geting older a year as past Masart is now six teen now he is not a mericl boy. But he stil is a grate mushishin.

Chapter 2

A lot of years have past. Mosart the champeant has gon to a restarnt he recuniesd some betey he oterd a budwiser a gow had pousin he put the pousin in his budwiser and left Mosart drinks it a nuther ower the master was bead the britun mushishin was bead. mosart the master how ever nos if a luther master will be better than Mosart.

Translation:

My Vision of Amadeus Mozart

A long time ago a genius was born and his family named him Mozart. He could play the piano. His sister Nanurl she was a genius too. One day Papa said, "We are going to England." Mozart and Nanurl they were extremely excited. Mozart and Nanurl never have been on a boat. At England at the palace the conductor said to the audience these children are a genius and watch and listen well. Mozart played the best and Nanurl did too. The audience called Mozart a miracle boy A couple of days after Mozart made his first symphony and then they went to Paris. And one day another musician came. Mozart felt so good that he is talking to a man that's a lot better than him. Nanurl was getting older and Mozart was too. Mozart made a Opera. Some people think his Papa is writing his music for him. One day a musician came to test Mozart. Afterwards the musician told the people in that town. So ever after the people know. No one doesn't think that Mozart's Papa doesn't write his music. Mozart was getting older. A year has passed. Mozart is now sixteen. Now he is not a miracle boy. But he is still a great musician.

Chapter 2

A lot of years have passed. Mozart the champion has gone to a restaurant. He recognized somebody. He ordered a Budweiser. A guy had poison. He put the poison in his Budweiser and left. Mozart drinks it. Another hour the master was dead. The brilliant musician was dead. Mozart the master. Who ever knows if another master will be better than Mozart.

Valiant effort; narrative power; keen interest; willingness to share; eagerness to try; courage to use big, lumpy, wobbly unstudied words; and vast, rumbling sound confusion! Three cheers for the author, and a life contract to his tutor.

Arrhythmias

Hesitant, halting, spurting, repetitive, or slushy speech is hard for a listener to follow; therefore, the two-way aspect of communication is automatically compromised.

Arrhythmic speech may reflect disruptions of thought. If the difficulty is word retrieval, target words are elusive. William James said that the absence of the sought-for word "creates an intensely active gap." One sufferer says, "Finding the right word is as satisfying and as specific as a big sneeze."

Katrina deHirsch, in her barrier-breaking study of arrhythmias, distinguished stuttering and cluttering—the latter being circular, repetitive, imprecise, "can't get to the point" speech: buckshot thought instead of bull's eye delivery. Remember the fellow in Chapter 2 who was trying to tell about buying cherry tomatoes? He's a clutterer. Always has been, always will be. Awkward retrieval, mixed with concern for using the exact word, has him dancing two steps backward for every three steps forward. Continuing the metaphor, sometimes his partner can't follow his lead.

People whose speech rhythm is jostled by slow retrieval usually have double trouble when they try to put their thoughts on paper. They may have excellent ideas but need extra time to set them down. If they should have even minor handwriting weaknesses, the "lethal cluster" effect will kick in. These problems, unnoticed and producing few negatives in elementary school, dampen academic success in the later years.

Teeth—absent or present, baby or adult—play a large part in articulation. Smooth articulation supports rhythmic speech.

Disorganization

Disorganized, sloppily slotted verbal intake—from either listening or reading—indicates a weakness in the language system. Chaotic output is also a danger sign, a symptom of language inefficiency or disability.

We have explored the important role of morphology in Chapter 2, and have frequently underscored the role time plays in organizing the file folders of memory and the forward thrust of Executive Function. An unsure sense of the concept of time is a major source of disorganization.

Chronophiles, holding time in high regard, use this linguistic tool to order their perceptions and experiences. *Chronophobes*, fearful and guilt-ridden at the prospect of tardiness, are driven to get things done on time. They like to arrive at the airport three hours before take-off, and they hand their term papers in early. Some unfortunate souls, *chrono-disabled*—suffering from *achronia*, try their best to muddle along but don't know what they're missing. These people are sending a warning signal.

Disorganized speaking mystifies and loses listeners; rambling writing bores readers and sends them to the coffee machine.

Inappropriate Behaviors

Weak language cuts kids off from social repartee. Particularly as they reach third grade and move up from there, social codes are dominated by language. Kids who cannot keep up, who don't get the joke, who ramble, or who clam up are on the rim of the action. Very often, in an attempt to catch up or deal themselves in, they turn to inappropriate behaviors. They may revert to baby talk, stage pratfalls, disrupt discipline, poke and prod, shout in people's ears, kick the cat, have sex, or take drugs.

Learning language is like climbing a staircase. Ascending, the climber with both feet on the same tread has sturdy balance. But, as one foot travels the riser heading for the next step, the climber is standing on only one foot—half the balance. If assaults, trauma, changes, or disruptions in the child's life coincide with a transition from one language level to the next, the child's newly acquired language skills may disintegrate. Faced with moving to a new house or apartment, the birth of a sibling, parental separation or divorce, death of a friend or relative, the child may teeter linguistically, and need to regress to an earlier level at which both feet can be solidly on the tread.

Children healing themselves in this manner must not be scolded, mocked, or admonished to grow up. They need to be understood, helped to consolidate, and given encouragement to continue the climb when they are ready. When a child whose language has been robust and ornamented slides backwards into primitive constructions, we may suspect unsettling events in the child's life, and do what we can to help.

This seems the place to mention again that language can often mitigate the social irritations of all children, including those with ADD. Weak language makes it harder for the child to check impulsivity. *Later, wait, the next turn, listen first—speak later* are behavioral brakes. Without them, impulse rules, and social disasters reign.

Misunderstandings

Weak language drains comprehension in listening and reading, and muddies output in speaking and writing. Here are some examples:

➻ Some concrete thinkers can manage short factual selections but become confused and irritated by abstraction. Simile, metaphor, figures of speech, or proverbs elude them.

127

•→ Some children with fragile language systems can manage small bits but not big chunks.

•→ Some "readers" can "word call" what's on the page but don't understand what they've read. They sound swell but can't answer questions later. That's why I put the word *reader* in quotes; they're not readers, they're callers.

Some stumbling readers for whom sound/symbol correspondence has been troublesome—or who have trouble keeping the chunks of polysyllabic words in order—labor so over decoding that there's not enough attentional energy left over for comprehension.

Forgetfulness

Forgetfulness is disruption. Recent research, reported in a *Fortune* magazine article reprinted by the Dana Alliance for Brain Research, divides memory into five types that we can remember through the acronym WIRES.

W stands for working memory, the ability to summon past knowledge, intuition, reasoning skills, and new information to work on a current problem or think about an issue. The associative skills of analogous thinking—language's highest abstraction—are vital here. The stronger the filing, retrieval, and associative systems, the more powerful the working memory.

I stands for implicit memory, which gives us the memory to ride a bike for the first time in several decades or to do Cat's Cradle. Language is incidental.

R stands for remote memory: name the five Great Lakes or the dates of the Civil War. Language is either a cut-off or a conduit for remote memory: rapid retrieval of target words, a strong sense of sequence, and efficient use of explanatory techniques. This is the memory sub-type called on in most tests and exams. And, although it's called "remote," this—combined with short-term, long-term, and working memory—is what we use for instructions, directions, and explanations.

E stands for episodic memory. How did you feel when everyone else was invited to the birthday party? Who figured out how to get the cat out of the tree? Where did you put your car in the parking lot? Which people came to the meeting, and who spoke out? This memory is heavily influenced by the emotional content of the episodes, and is also intimately connected to what physicists and others who escape the limitations of time call "memory of the future"—amplified anticipation. Language makes episodic memory powerful or powerless.

S stands for semantic memory, remembering what words mean. Obviously, this can't exist without language.

By looking at different kinds of memory, we can see how power strengthens or weakness undercuts actions and words.

Malapropisms, Spoonerisms, and Galimatias

Malapropisms and Spoonerisms come from switching sounds around, for example interchanging *progeny* and *prodigy*, or referring to the *queer old dean* as the *dear old queen*. Galimatias, according to my dictionary, is confused or unintelligible talk—gibberish. These inaccuracies, common in very young children but markers of distress from roughly first grade on, result in language which is, in East Texas talk, *"a half bubble off plumb."*

Here are a few masterpieces of miasma, my *pique experiences.*

The fifth grader wrote for the school newspaper, "Our soccer team was *underfeeted.*"

Five-year-old Melissa said, "Granny, I can swim. I can swim the *dog pedal.*"

The psychologist said to the group of new teachers, "Eye contact is *exhaustive.*"

Writing a year-end report, the kindergarten teacher said of Jenny, "She has an *innane* curiosity."

Of fourth grader Edward, the teacher wrote, "He seems sad much of the time, and disagreeable. He's quite *remorse.* Yesterday, he was totally *disgrunted.*" (*morose, disgruntled*).

Second grader SaraBeth said, "My Mom's car is in the *drivement.*"

Today, as I was working on this chapter, I received this confirmation letter from a hotel where I have booked a room:

Dear Madam,
You are hereby confirmed as a non-smoking Queen.

So what are we supposed to do about all this?

1. Have a thorough hearing check-up for all children who show any symptom of language weakness. Arrange a language evaluation if indicated. It's never too early.

2. Help children enjoy wordplay, moving in this sequence: copy, recognize, select, create. If we were practicing rhyming, for example, we could say:

"Copy the rhymes I say: *run* and *fun, sad* and *glad, jump* and *bump.*"

"Do these words rhyme: *marmalade* and *jelly?*"

"Which pair of words rhymes: *chair/bear* or *chair/table?*"

"Make a rhyme for the word *night.*"

"Make up a pair of rhyming words."

3. Build in a "logic alarm system" to warn of galimatias: let kids *see* what speech *looks like.* I think of fourth grader David, who was a passionate verbal defender of what he called *ininjured species.* No one could get him to say *endangered* until we wrote out the word *danger,* and discussed it. We then wrote *endanger* and talked some more, finally getting to *endangered.* After that, he could always spell it correctly, but the spoken habit of *ininjured* was too strong to overcome, and since it made sense in its own way, we let it slide.

4. Help dysnomic kids organize their thoughts before trying to write or speak them. Train them to collect their list of vital facts, names, places, and dates on an index card, ready for quick consultation. Later, they can ask permission to take such a card with them to a test or exam.

5. Arrhythmic kids often need extra time. Provide it. Teach them the experience and joys of fluency through song and poetry.

6. Use role playing to help kids move beyond inappropriate social behavior.

7. Prime the pump for comprehension, showing kids how to predict what a story or article will be about. Help them "activate prior knowledge" as a way of bringing their own thoughts to the foreground. They can then slot new information alongside what they already understand.

8. Show kids how to use visualization and repetition as memory aids. The supermarket is an ideal place. Say a list of items to children, ask them to see the items in their minds' eyes as you say them, then see how many they can bring back. Teach them to repeat the list as another memory aid.

visualization

9. To separate verbal gaffes from true language, introduce children from second grade up to such characters as Amelia Bedelia and such books as *The King Who Rained*. Once they get the joke, they see the point.

10. Collect proverbs, figures of speech, and idiomatic sayings. Put each one on a piece of poster board and let kids make illustrations. Children with innately weak language don't understand these constructions. The way they interpret and use language is—in the words of the Chinese proverb—"like climbing a tree to catch a fish."

Our family favorite is "Trust your Mother, but cut the cards"—close cousin to the Arab "Trust in God, but tie your camel." What would they make of "The son of a duck is a floater?"

And now, since "Fine words butter no parsnips," it's time for Chapter 10, Ten Commandments.

Ten Commandments

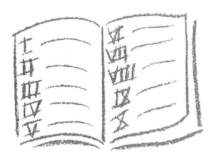

1. Nurture receptive language: plant well. Then, tend and harvest expressive language crops. "As ye sow, so shall ye reap."

2. Encourage *active* listening and reading.

3. Writing and speaking needn't be lengthy and flowery to be good; pithy packs a punch. Precise terminology is clear. Labels focus. Verbs propel. Adjectives and adverbs create pauses. Choose accordingly.

precise terminology

4. Teach and model the use of language to mediate behavior.

5. Play with words, relish language, encourage experimentation, spread this benevolent contagion.

6. Use the 6 *wh* words, the terminology of Executive Function, and other organizational aids for efficient filing, smooth retrieval, and delivery to the convergence zone. Catalogue vocabulary. Play "word sprints," in which kids see how many things they can name which belong in the kitchen. How many

wh words

kinds of sports equipment? Precision grows with practice. Label the ladle; let wire whisk replace "thingy."

7. Teach organization in time and space:

∘⊸ **Time**

a) Using index cards and notebook rings, help each kid make a Days of the Week ring and a Months of the Year ring. The act of writing out the names—and adding small illustrations—will help the information stick. The students will readily see that the sequence is always the same.

Use color: write the names of the weekdays in red and the names of the weekend days in blue. Write the names of the winter months in gray, the spring months in green or yellow, the summer months in blue, and the fall months in orange or brown. Save time for children to add their own illustrations. Use these time rings to play games about what comes *before*, *after*, or *in between*.

b) At home and at school, have a large calendar showing at least three months at a time. Color code it for recurrent activities and special days. At the end of each day, ask one child to put a little illustration of what happened that day on the appropriate square. This will provide a visual reminder of physical experiences arranged on a time line.

Then, help the children mentally travel back and forth. How many days last week did it rain? How many birthdays coming this month? How long untill we go to the Science Museum? Walking the time line reinforces the invisible concept of the linear nature of time.

c) Probe each child's comprehension of time. Take nothing for granted. Teach what's missing.

d) Model ways to use the concept of time to plan, carry on, and finish.

e) Show kids how to measure and monitor their concentration spans. Ask them to look at the clock and start reading something they enjoy. The instant they lose their concentration, they look at the clock again. How much time has passed? Do this five or ten times. Make an average. Do the same thing with material that's hard. Measure in the same way. Then, like strengthening muscles, can they extend their span by a minute or two...or five? Kids who concentrate well for ten minutes are better off working in three ten-minute segments than trying to glue themselves to the chair for half an hour.

f) Offer practice in doing something "for ten minutes," etc. Knowing the feeling of elapsing time is a treasure of great worth during tests and exams.

g) Keep an analog clock on display. Seeing the hands go around reinforces the concept of the circular nature of time. Incidentally, Rolls Royce uses analog clocks because they are so easy to read at a glance.

h) Speak in the precise language of time, instead of in harried generalities of lateness: "We need to leave for the library in fifteen minutes. You have a nice bit of time to finish what you're doing." vs. "Oh, my Lord, how did it get so late? Hurry up. We don't have time for that now."

i) Listen for the presence or absence of verb tenses and endings. If absent, model. If they don't stick, get an evaluation and help.

j) Let kids make their own versions of "Time Magazine." Here are some sample pages. Add others according to need or interest.

Page 1. **My Clock**

Using a paper plate, a brad, and two hands cut from construction paper, make a clock face. Write the hours in green on the inside rim, and the minutes in red on the outside rim. Make the little hand out of green paper, the big hand out of red. Each hand reads its own color, and the little hand speaks first.

Page 2. **How To Tell Time**

There are twelve "hour names" in every day. There are 60 minutes in every hour and 60 seconds in every minute. A digital clock shows the hour, then :, then the minutes. An analog clock has two hands: the little hand names the hours, the big hand names the minutes. The little hand speaks first. For instance, it might be 3:30. Make your paper clock show that. When the big hand is exactly at 60, it is a new "o'clock." We say the number the little hand shows and "o'clock." Make your clock show six o'clock.

Page 3. **Parts of the Day**

Every day has different sections, just as every year has different seasons. From sunrise until 12:00 is called *morning*. Write here the things you do in the morning:

From 12:00—which is also called *noon*—until twilight is called *afternoon*. Figure out why. Write here the things you do in the afternoon:

Page 4. From twilight until you go to bed is called *evening*. Write here what you like to do in the evening:

From when it gets dark until it gets light again is called *night*. Write here what you do at night:

What is your favorite time of day?

Please tell why.

Page 5. AM and PM

The hour hand goes all the way around the dial twice in each complete day. The letters AM stand for the trip around the dial between 12:00 midnight and 12:00 noon. The initials PM stand for the trip around the dial between noon and midnight. On timetables, the PM times are often printed in darker ink. Paste a timetable here:

Page 6. My Personal Timetable

In the morning:

I get up at _____ o'clock.

I eat breakfast at _____ o'clock.

I leave for school at _____ o'clock.

Then:

I eat lunch at _____ o'clock.

I come home at _____ o'clock.

I eat supper at _____ o'clock.

I usually fall asleep around _____ o'clock.

Page 7. More Timetable Facts About Me

(whole page free for kid to fill in)

Page 8. Lengths of Time

It takes me _____ minutes to eat breakfast.

It takes me _____ minutes to walk a mile.

It takes me _____ minutes to get dressed.

It takes me _____ minutes to eat a candy bar.

It takes _____ minutes to get to school.

My favorite TV show starts at _____ o'clock, and ends at _____ o'clock.

It lasts _____ minutes.

It takes me _____ minutes to: (kid's choice)

Page 9. Passing Time

Time probably seems to pass VERY slowly when you are bored, tired, sick, or can't move around. Time probably seems to pass VERY quickly when you feel good and are busy having fun. List here the different things you do:

Time goes quickly when I'm:

Time goes slowly when I'm:

Page 10. **Stop the Clock**

If all the clocks in all the world were going to stop at one time, I would pick _____ o'clock because: (whole page for kid to do)

○━ **Space**

a) Arrange consistent workplaces.

b) Teach children to preview the materials they'll need, locate them, and have them ready *before* starting to work.

c) Have a designated destination for completed work.

d) Provide colored folders for different kinds of work—one pocket holding "to do," the other holding "work in progress."

e) Explain to parents the importance of a designated work space at home.

f) Explain why each kid needs a backpack into which all schoolwork goes.

g) Give assignment pads with big pages and good spaces between the lines. Three-inch by five-inch spiral-bounds lead to cramped, illegible writing.

⊶ Time and Space

The late Harriet Sheridan, Dean of the College at Brown University, used to say that organization in time and space are handy in elementary school, supportive in middle school, vital in high school, and prerequisite to success in college. That being the case, she said, start as soon as possible. She further stated that the difference between kids who make it in college and those who don't depends on whether they can orient themselves and their work in time and space.

She recommended that parents, teachers, and students work out a treaty involving when and where work is to be done—taking the kids' preferences into account. After all agree, they shake hands. Everyone is required to honor the treaty for six weeks. It can be re-negotiated after that time. This seems a benevolent tyranny.

8. Screen kids' language at third grade—or later if it hasn't already been done. Why then? Third grade is the time when language normally shifts into subtler, more abstract levels. We need to know if the child is OK. A screening would include:

⊶ comprehension of time

⊶ ability to define a word

⊶ understanding figures of speech

⊶ explaining how two objects are the same and different

⊶ skills of segmentation and syllable arrangement. (The best way to test this is to give a trial lesson in Pig Latin. Kids who can do it are on to a new code. Those who struggle are revealing their needs.)

One administrator asked, "Why not give it in second grade and get ahead of the game?" To me, that's like scheduling a corn-on-the-cob speed-eating contest for first graders: their teeth aren't in yet! We glean the most information by screening for the presence or absence of those abilities which belong to a particular age.

9. Enlist parents' help. Show them what matters. Teach them to correct by modeling: hearing, translating into correct construction, giving back. Ask them to notice what sticks and what doesn't. Encourage them to be willing to seek help.

10. Cavort with some linguistically high-level hijinks. Soar and enjoy!

Conclusion
The Innkeeper

At the service to install Terence Elsberry as the new rector of our church, his mentor, John Harper, gave a short sermon likening the job of the priest to the job of the innkeeper. I found myself thinking that educators, parents, and other concerned adults share the same obligations and opportunities.

In the words of the sermon, the good innkeeper's tasks are to:

- tend the fire
- offer sustenance
- tell the story.

Tend the fire. Using language, let us strike the spark of enthusiasm, kindle curiosity, care for the light of learning, work the bellows of exchange, lay on the logs of concepts, and gather around the hearth of knowledge as we share the warmth of enjoyment.

Offer sustenance. Through words, let us give food for thought as replenishment to the hungry, as evidence of hospitality and welcome to a community of learners, and as nourishment for new growth. Sustenance includes information, strategies, opportunities, new chances, and delight in discovery.

Tell the story. Sharing past, present, and future through the miracle of language, people of all ages tell the stories of who we are, what we're doing, where we've come from, and where we're going. Our stories shape other lives, just as theirs shape ours.

Language is the passepartout—the key which enables the traveler to open the doors and discover the possibilities and delights inside the inn. But, doors, as we know, work both ways. After providing warmth and shelter, the innkeeper's final job is to help travelers go out and on their way—to explore new realms and reach their destinations.

Bon voyage.

Pax vobiscum.

Resource Section

Three Organizations

Modern Learning Press/Programs for Education, Box 167, Rosemont, NJ 08556 (1-800-627-5867). This excellent publishing house offers a wide variety of wholly reliable, exciting materials for educators and parents. They are a welcome resource.

Educators Publishing Service, 31 Smith Place, Cambridge, MA 02138. This publisher offers multi-sensory and organizational materials, originally designed for dyslexics, which work magnificently in regular classrooms. The descriptions and age/grade levels in their catalogues are scrupulously fair.

The Orton Dyslexia Society, Chester Building, Suite 382, 8600 LaSalle Rd., Baltimore, MD 21204-6020. This organization brings together physicians, researchers, educators, and parents, offering excellent publications and conferences open to any interested participant.

General Bibliography

Priscilla Vail's books

(available at bookstores or from Modern Learning Press—see above)

About Dyslexia: Unraveling the Myth. Rosemont, NJ: Modern Learning Press/Programs for Education, 1990.

Clear & Lively Writing: Language Games and Activities for Everyone. New York: Walker & Co., 1981.

Common Ground: Whole Language and Phonics Working Together. Rosemont, NJ: Modern Learning Press/Programs for Education, 1991.

Emotion. The On/Off Switch for Learning. Rosemont, NJ: Modern Learning Press/ Programs for Education, 1994.

Gifted, Precocious, or Just Plain Smart. Rosemont, NJ: Modern Learning Press/ Programs for Education, 1987.

Learning Styles: Food for Thought and 130 Practical Tips. Rosemont, NJ: Modern Learning Press/Programs for Education, 1992.

Smart Kids With School Problems: Things to Know and Ways to Help. New York: NAL Plume Paperback, 1989.

The World of the Gifted Child. New York: Walker & Co., 1979 (currently between printings, available through libraries).

Other Authors and Titles

Erikson, Erik. *Childhood & Society.* New York: W.W. Norton, 1950.

Fraiberg, Selma. *The Magic Years.* New York: Charles Scribner's Sons, 1959.

Galaburda, Albert. *From Reading to Neurons.* Cambridge, MA: MIT Press, 1989.

Gardner, Howard. *Frames of Mind: the Theory of Multiple Intelligences.* New York: Basic Books, 1984.

Hallowell, Edward M., and Thompson, Michael G. *Finding the Heart of the Child.* Braintree, MA: Association of Independent Schools of Massachusetts, 1993.

Hallowell, Edward M., and Ratey, John J. *Driven to Distraction: Attention Deficit Disorder in Children and Adults.* New York: Pantheon Books, 1994.

Healy, Jane M. *Your Child's Growing Mind.* New York: Doubleday, 1987.

Healy, Jane M. *Endangered Minds.* New York: Doubleday, 1989.

Henry, Marcia. *Words.* Los Gatos, CA: Lex Press.

deHirsch, Katrina. *Language and the Developing Child.* Baltimore: the Orton Dyslexia Society, Monograph #4, 1984.

Levine, Mel. *Keeping a Head in School.* Cambridge, MA: Educator's Publishing Service, 1990.

Luria, A. *The Mind of Mnemonist.* Cambridge, MA: Harvard University Press, 1968.

MacNeil, Robert. *Wordstruck.* New York: Penguin Books, 1989.

Pinker, Steven. *The Language Instinct.* New York: William Morrow, 1994.

Rawson, Margaret. *The Many Faces of Dyslexia.* Baltimore: Orton Dyslexia Society, 1989.

Restak, Richard. *The Brain Has a Mind of Its Own.* New York: Crown, 1991.

Rosner, Jerome. *Helping Children Overcome Learning Difficulties.* New York: Walker & Co., 1980.

Schafer, Edith N. *Our Remarkable Memory.* Washington and Philadelphia: Starrhill Press, 1988.

Seligman, Martin E.P. *The Optimistic Child.* New York: Knopf, 1981.

Sizer, Theodore R. *Horace's School.* Boston: Houghton Mifflin Co., 1992.

Vygotsky, Lev. *Thought & Language.* Cambridge, MA: MIT Press, 1962.

Source Notes & References By Chapter

Chapter 1
#1 *Webster's New International Dictonary.*

#2 Miller, George and Patricia Gildea. "How Children Learn Words," *Scientific American,* September, 1987.

#3 Epstein, Herman. "Multimodality, Crossmodality & Dyslexia," *Annals of Dyslexia,* 1985.

Chapter 3
#1 Renzulli, Joseph, and Sally Reis, *The Schoolwide Enrichment Model.*

#2 Erikson, Erik. *Childhood & Society.*

Chapter 4
#1 Vygotsky, Lev. *Thought & Language.*

Chapter 5
#1 MacNeil, Robert. *Wordstruck.*

#2 Conkling, Grace. *The Whole Duty of Berkshire Brooks.*

Chapter 7
#1 Cox, Aylett. Spoken at an address to the Orton Dyslexia Society, 1981.

#2 and #3 Wordsworth, William. "Evening on Calais Beach" and "Daffodils."

#4 Carson, Anne. "On Chronoluminism," *Plainwater.*

#5 D'Amasio, Antonio. *Descartes' Error: Emotion, Reason and the Human Brain.*

Chapter 8
#1 Hallowell, Edward and Michael Thompson. *Finding the Heart of the Child.*

Chapter 9
#1 Zvi, Jennifer, Learning Disabilities Specialist and Ph.D. at California State University in Northridge, CA.

Index

A
allergies 60, 76, 81, 86
analogy 16, 90, 96, 103
Attention Deficit Disorder 107, 109, 127

B
behavior 39, 40, 48, 53, 65, 99, 106–107, 126, 132, 133

C
children 1, 2, 3, 6, 7, 11, 12, 35, 37, 53, 56, 57
comparison 90, 95

D
description 74, 94–95
dyslexia 38, 53, 60, 62

E
emotional development 27, 35
expressive language 6, 14, 16, 18, 25, 40, 120, 122, 133

G
Galaburda, Albert 30
Gardner, Howard 28
gifted 30, 31

H
Hallowell, Edward 103

I
intellectual development 27, 28–35

K
Kaufman, Alan & Nadine 29

L
language 1–8, 10–13, 15, 17–18, 20–22, 24–26, 28, 30–32, 34–35, 37, 40–41, 46, 50, 54, 55, 59, 62–73, 99, 101–106, 117–121, 125–129, 132, 135, 140
listening 8, 15, 14, 17, 26, 32, 39, 45–50, 48, 50, 51, 73, 104, 108, 114, 123, 125, 127, 133, 135
Luria, A.R. 29

M

memory 17, 20, 37, 47–50, 52, 60, 90, 100, 104, 111, 113, 126, 128, 129, 132
morphology 17, 21, 95, 126

O

organization 7, 21, 25, 32, 41, 58, 61, 115, 121, 134, 140

P

parents 5, 11, 14, 18, 23, 36, 39, 42, 46, 54, 60, 67, 101, 102, 110, 114, 118, 139

Q

questions 10, 16, 22, 26, 30, 43, 50, 54, 57, 105, 114, 128

R

reading 5, 6, 15, 20, 24, 26, 31, 33, 42, 43, 45, 50–55, 63, 69, 71, 73, 74, 76, 80, 82, 84, 85, 102–104, 108, 119, 125, 127, 133, 135
receptive language 13–16, 122, 133
Renzulli, Joseph 30

S

semantics 17, 22
Sizer, Theodore 31
speaking 24, 45, 55, 62, 70, 78, 80, 87, 82, 103, 108, 131, 135
Specific Language Disability 43, 62, 122
speech 7, 8, 15, 16, 23, 25, 55–57, 71, 82, 86, 121, 124, 125, 127, 131, 132, 140
students 2, 3, 9, 28, 30, 38, 40, 42, 51, 54, 58, 59, 61, 62, 70, 71, 75, 92, 94, 98, 104, 109, 113, 115, 134, 140
syntax 11, 17, 22, 121

T

teachers 5, 9, 11, 19, 23, 30, 33, 38, 42, 46, 54, 59, 60–62, 72, 75, 81, 85, 92, 112, 130, 140
time 11, 25, 26, 46, 54, 59, 62, 66, 70, 71, 77–79, 84, 94, 95, 97, 100, 104, 111–115, 125, 129, 131, 134, 140

V

vocabulary 6–9, 32, 34, 39, 42, 69, 74, 79, 90, 92–96, 103, 107, 121, 133
Vygotsky, Lev 7, 57

W

words 5, 6, 7, 8, 9, 15, 16, 18, 20, 21, 22, 24, 25, 32, 33, 34, 35, 39, 40, 41, 42, 43, 46, 47, 51, 53, 56, 57, 61, 62, 73, 76, 77, 79, 84, 86, 90, 98, 103, 104, 107, 108, 113, 115, 119, 120, 124, 131, 133, 140
writing 6, 7, 24, 26, 31, 35, 41, 45, 57–61, 65, 71, 74, 80, 82, 92, 94, 103, 104, 108, 110, 112, 113, 121, 122, 125, 126, 127, 131, 133, 134, 136, 139